MAKING
CONNECTIONS
Around the World with Log Cabin

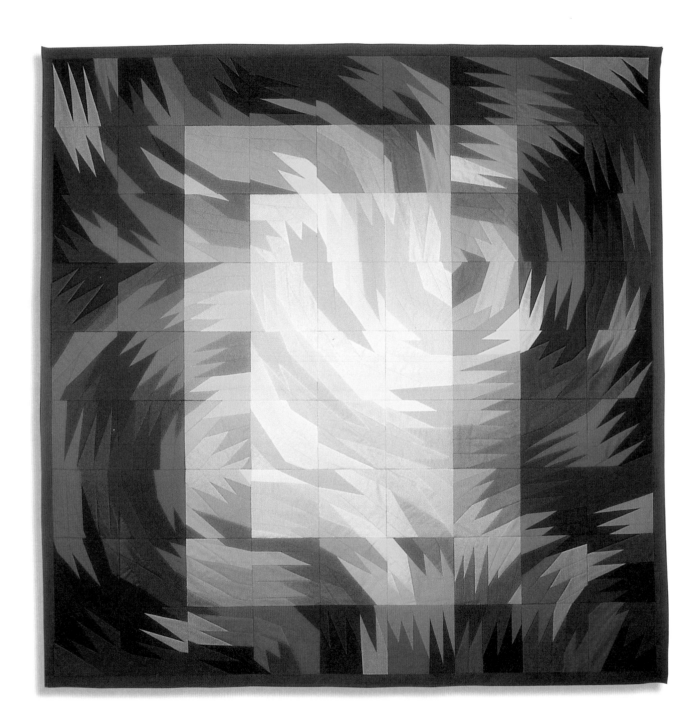

'Life Force', 1995
Barbara Macey, Australia
138cm (55in) square

MAKING CONNECTIONS

Around the World with Log Cabin

Janet Rae and Dinah Travis

RT Publishing TR

Making Connection: Around the World with Log Cabin
first published in Great Britain in 2004 by
RT Publishing
36 Beech Avenue, Chartham,
England CT4 7TA.

Text and design Copyright © 2004
Janet Rae and Dinah Travis

All rights reserved

No part of this book may be reproduced or transmitted by
any process without the written permission of the publisher.

Book layout and production by
eidetic, 5 West Stanhope Place, Edinburgh EH12 5HQ

Printed in the UK by
CPI Group

ISBN 0 9547459 0 6

Cover:
Detail, stripes and tartan quilt,
Scotland, c.1900
©Perth Museum & Art Gallery

CONTENTS

PREFACE

The Log Cabin patchwork pattern is as popular today among quiltmakers as it was in the latter part of the 19th century. Intrigued by its endless permutations, many contemporary textile artists around the world have pushed the design in ways which would have astounded the early users of the pattern: not the Victorians who often embellished their silk and satin Log Cabin blocks with embroidery and even paint, but the frugal homemakers who had to recycle worn clothing and bed linen.

Other contemporary artists too – whether by choice or happenstance – have used the pattern as the basis of their work. One of the most curious is *Bed* by Robert Rauschenberg in the Museum of Modern Art, New York. Here a Log Cabin quilt is used as the canvas – simply because it was close to the artist's hand when inspiration struck. More graphic and brightly coloured expressions of the pattern can be found in the work of Frank Stella (*Hyena Stomp* 1962)– see page 63 - and Eduardo Paolozzi (*Tapestry* 1966). Both works are in Tate Modern, London.

'Log Cabin' is an American title and American mythology explains that the strips of the block are logs: the red centre a fire, and the traditional light and dark sides the shadows thrown by the fire (a yellow centre in the block has also been defined as the lighted window of a log cabin.) In this book, Log Cabin is used to denote a broad family of work which relies on the use of strips – and because the name has become generic through popular usage and is easily recognisable to contemporary quiltmakers around the globe. In the British Isles, it has been given several labels. *The Girl's Own Paper* of 18 February 1882 called it Canadian or Loghouse quilt patchwork, as did the 1885 edition of The *Dictionary of Needlework* by Sophia Caulfield and Blanche Saward, published in both London and Paris. The latter gave directions for making the blocks with overlapping ribbons sewn to a ground. In 1886, Volume 1 (No. 5) of *Weldon's Practical Patchwork* also gave instructions for a 'Ribbon Patchwork' (Fig 1) which in the present day might be called Chevron Log Cabin – but with strips sewn over papers in the traditional English manner.

By Volume 3 (No. 30), *Weldon's* was showing two different illustrations of Log Cabin: one was called Canadian or Loghouse Patchwork and the other American Log Patchwork. (Fig 2) *Weldon's* noted the difference thus:

> *'American patchwork, or Log-house quilting as it is called in Canada, differs from ordinary patchwork in that the sections are cut in strips and instead of being sewn are run one upon the other from the central square and turned down, so no stitches are visible.'*

Fig 1: Ribbon patchwork from Weldon's Practical Patchwork Vol 1(No 5).

Fig 2: The American (left) and Canadian illustrations showing the editor's concept of differences in pattern appeared in Vol 3 (no 30).

Canadian or Loghouse Patchwork was described as

'... a variation of American patchwork, and is executed with strips to form squares, but the colours are arranged in such a manner that when finished each block appears as if made of four angles of a diamond, intersected by long bars passing in the centre one over the other, like wicker work.'

If this caused confusion, then terminology became all the more complex by 1897, when other names were being suggested for the pattern in other British publications. Mary Whitley, who edited *Every Girl's Book of Sport, Occupation and Pastime*, after calling it Canadian Logwood, suggested that it would be more appropriate to call it the Egyptian or Mummy pattern (see page 12), while in 1910 M.K. Gifford's book, *Needlework*, called it Straight Patchwork. She commented:

'The pattern has been carried out to Canada, where, made with ribbons instead of calicoes, it gained favour and was called the "log cabin" design, though it is suggestive of parquetry rather than of logs.'

On the Isle of Man, it is called the Roof Pattern and in Canada, the 'family' of the Log Cabin quilt is extended to include all related strip patterns. Collector and author Ruth McKendry (*Quilts and Other Bed Coverings in the Canadian Tradition*, Van Nostrand Reinhold 1979) says: 'Possibly fence rail and chevron should not be included but various traditional quilters have told me that any quilts made with logs or strips are called log cabin quilts.'(1)

In America, the pattern is linked to the second presidential campaign of Abraham Lincoln in 1864 (2). Some extant Log Cabin quilts in both Europe and America date from slightly earlier but of course log cabins had special significance for Lincoln – as the place of his birth. Perhaps 1864 indicates the date when Americans adopted the title for this particular block? Certainly the title subsequently crossed back over the Atlantic to Europe, but not the pattern itself – it was already there. One of the characteristics of the American flowering of patchwork and quilting in the mid and late 19th centuries was the naming of patchwork blocks – often with patriotic, symbolic, religious or political themes. It was a practice not generally followed in Europe, especially in Britain where geometric descriptions generally ruled the day.

The source of the Log Cabin block and its associated 'family' is a long and interesting trail going back to at least the first century AD. In this book it is looked at in the wider context of associated patterns and influences – an investigation of design history which links past and present. Hopefully, the Log Cabin story also challenges the future – and especially those contemporary quiltmakers and textile artists who like to push traditional boundaries.

FOOTNOTES:
1. Private correspondence dated 12 april 2003. NB The term 'Chevron' is used here to describe the type of quilt shown on page 73.
2. Page 170, *Clues in the Calico* by Barbara Brackman. EPM Publications Inc, 1989.

Turkey Red and white Log Cabin,
Scotland, c.1870
203 x 207cm (80 x 82in)
Author's Collection
(Photo by Michael Wicks)

PATTERN SOURCES

■

Attempting to trace the origins of the Log Cabin pattern calls for patience. Just when you think you have nailed down its source, the 'sand shifts', another avenue of research presents itself and you are forced to step back a few hundred years further to examine yet another culture. The intrigue lies in its antiquity and its varying applications to different crafts – not only textiles. The enigma of the Log Cabin family of patterns is their appearance in diverse countries around the globe. It is a pattern that has travelled across oceans and through time: sometimes the routes and carriers can be explained, but often there remains only speculation.

A very primitive yet related form of the pattern, for example, appears on a piece of pre-Hispanic pottery in the Gold Museum in Lima, Peru (Fig 3). Originating from the coastal Paracas culture, the pottery is decorated with a series of irregular rectangles within rectangles. Interestingly they are coloured in red, black and gold – the gold being reserved for the centre rectangle. When the Spaniard Francisco Pizarro marched to confront the

Fig 3: Drawing of incised rectangles on a pre-Hispanic pot made in Peru. (Gold Museum, Lima)

last Incan ruler in 1532, Peru was already a highly civilised empire with monumental architecture (contemporary with the pyramids in Egypt) and highly developed pottery, textile and gold working skills. In addition to pottery, Paracas was also an established centre for textile weaving. Its fine fabrics were often used to denote high status and given as royal gifts – also to wrap mummies. Textiles and pottery from Paracas were decorated with rough geometric forms including the key, sawtooth, spiral, hexagon, rectangle and square.

A much later example of the Log Cabin pattern, with a more ready attribution, can be seen in the Auckland Institute and Museum in New Zealand and in particular within a display of Cook Islands 'Household Equipment'. A Pandanus woven mat sampler from Aitutaki includes a simple off-centre Log Cabin block executed in red dating from about 1926. (Fig 4) The same display case also includes a patchwork cushion cover in the same design made in red, white, green and yellow cotton. It came into the museum collection in 1932 but when it was made is unknown. (Fig 5) When we learn that the London Missionary Society became active in the Cook Islands (or Hervey Islands as they were called then) in the 1820s, the pattern's progress to the Pacific from Europe is readily explained. Founded in 1795, in the wake of England's evangelical revival, the Society's main objective was to spread the knowledge of Christ among heathen and other unenlightened peoples. Its first successful mission to Tahiti in 1797 was quickly followed by other voyages to islands in the South Pacific with missionaries who not only carried the gospel but also taught reading and writing and European-based skills such as patchwork. The skill of making

Fig 4
Detail of woven mat sampler from the Cook Islands. (Auckland Institute & Museum)

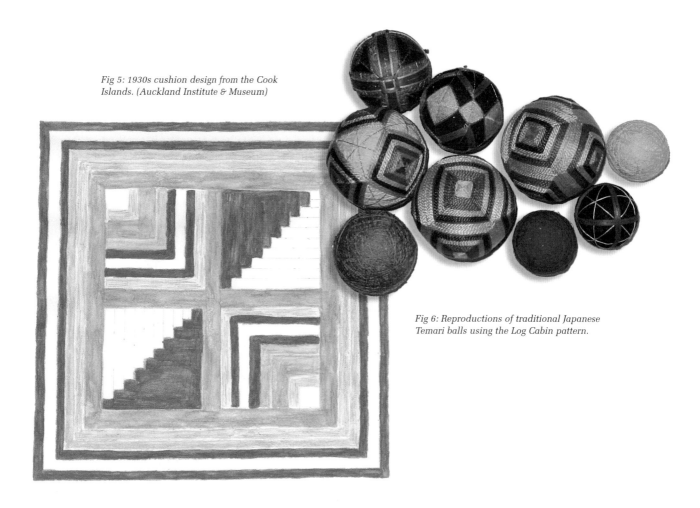

Fig 5: 1930s cushion design from the Cook Islands. (Auckland Institute & Museum)

Fig 6: Reproductions of traditional Japanese Temari balls using the Log Cabin pattern.

patchwork, brought by the missionaries to the Cook Islands, remains a distinctive inheritance to the present day.

But, to take the pattern mystery to yet another culture, consider the geometric designs used on the traditional Temari or thread balls of Japan. (Fig 6) These embroidered balls are thought to be pre-16th century and had many uses: one suggestion is that they originally encased herbs and were made by ladies of the court; another that they were children's toys; still another has them used as good luck charms. Whatever their purpose, they were highly ornamental and employed a variety of geometric designs. Executed first in silk threads and later in cotton, their many variations include distinct 'relatives' of the Log Cabin pattern – strips around a centre square.

And, what influenced the French cabinetmaker Bernard II van Risenburgh in 1735 to use a form of Log Cabin (today it might be called 'string' or chevron patchwork) in his oak cabinet veneered with a number of exotic woods? (Fig 7) (See the related quilt on page 73). The cabinet is in the Collection of The J. Paul Getty Museum, Los

Angeles and is some 15 feet in length. It features six doors with gilt-bronze mounts: four doors have bell-like shapes filled with Log Cabin squares on point while the remaining two doors have an unusual cornucopia-like design, again with squares on point. Many fine examples of 18th and 19th century French and English veneered furniture decorated with geometric designs survive in museums and stately homes. And, one might also spot examples of the splendid geometric marble mosaic tabletops made by Italians in the 16th and 17th centuries.

The pattern known as 'box' (in patchwork 'tumbling blocks') was a particular favourite of wood inlay craftsmen and, together with diamonds, strips, triangles and other geometric forms, became the distinguishing feature of the 'new' process of making cheaper wood mosaic developed in Tunbridge, England, about 1820. Whereas craftsmen had previously cut individual pieces of veneer to form sheets of marquetry, the new practice of assembling contrasting wood sticks according to a graphed design, then slicing them across, meant that it was possible to produce multiples – whether

Fig 7: Close-up of inlaid cabinet panel in the collection of The J. Paul Getty Museum, Los Angeles. It was made in France by Bernard II van Risenburgh in 1735. (© The J. Paul Getty Museum)

Fig 8: Embroidered geometric patterns on the back of a mid 17th century casket. (©The Trustees of the National Museums of Scotland)

geometric or pictorial. Tunbridge Ware, executed on a wide variety of objects, from tables to pin boxes and tea caddies to cribbage boards, climbed to such ornamental heights that it even embraced complex Berlin wool patterns in its repertoire. And yet, speaking solely of the Log Cabin pattern in relation to this flurry of geometric wood ornamentation, the van Risenburgh cabinet remains unusual.

Although existing Log Cabin quilts usually date from the mid 19th century, we do know that the Log Cabin pattern was used as an embroidery stitch in England from 1650. A square perfume bag, worked in latticed silks (a 'sachet a parfum en treillis et fils de soie, Angleterre - 1650-1670') with the Cross formation mentioned on page 31, is illustrated in *Domestic Needlework* by G. Saville Seligman and E. Talbot Hughes (London, Country Life, 1926). And, the National Museums of Scotland hold an exquisite embroidered casket (Fig 8) of the same period. The casket, which is either English or Scottish, includes the Log Cabin pattern as one of its decorative stitches on the back, the front being embroidered with figurative scenes. Its contents are an amazing collection of sewing tools, and secret drawers with purses, and collections of small 'toys' (animals made out of silver metal coiled thread). Only a few such caskets remain in museum collections, and it is believed they were made by young girls who first

embroidered a linen or satin ground and then applied the work to a wooden case (1). How did these young embroideresses and the other craft workers come to use the pattern?

◼

Weaving and the Egyptian Link

To fully understand the antiquity of the Log Cabin pattern it is necessary to step back in time well before the 16th century and to its early appearance in the wrappings of Egyptian mummies. Here, however, the pattern was *woven* as opposed to sewn, painted or etched and Egyptologists put its use to a certain period of time – Egypt's Roman period that extended from 30 BC to AD 395. This despite the fact that mummification as a practice is believed to have started as early as 3000 BC.

During the Roman period, the complexity of the linen mummy wrappings moved on from simple swathing bandages to the use of recognisable patterns – in particular the rhomboid and variations of what we call the Log Cabin. This perhaps explains why Mary Whitley, editor of *Every Girl's Book of Sport, Occupation and Pastime*, called the pattern in 1897 'Mummy or Egyptian Patchwork' as an alternative to 'Canadian Logwood' and referred her readers to numerous examples of mummies on exhibit in the British, Oxford and other museums. Taken in the context of the period, it is important to remember that the British Museum, founded by an Act of Parliament in 1753, began receiving Egyptian artefacts into its collection in 1801 as spoils of war. During the occupation of Alexandria, Napoleon had directed his army to assemble ancient Egyptian artefacts for removal to France. However, before they could be moved, the French were forced to surrender to British troops and the 'cache' was instead taken to England. It included the famous Rosetta Stone and the sarcophagus claimed to have been the tomb of Alexander. Certainly by 1862, the British public was long conversant with ancient Egyptian history and artefacts: Samuel Sharpe, who compiled a detailed catalogue of the British Museum's Egyptian holdings (2) at the time, described the display area as extensive – extending through a long gallery on the ground floor, up the staircase to the first floor, onto the landing and into two other rooms. Another chronicler of the Museum's history, Henry Charles Shelly (3), noted that there was nearly 50,000 items in the Museum's collection of ancient Egypt and that while Egyptology was still in its infancy, 'it was as catching as measles'.

A number of examples of the more decorative swathing exist. National Museums of Scotland have three mummies with bandaging in the rhomboid style – two men and a child. (Fig 9) All date from the Roman period and are from excavations at Hawara. Of particular interest is the ornamentation – a gold foil wrapped or brass stud has been placed in the centre of each rhomboid. Portraits on panels or sculpted heads together with gilding are another of the ornamental features. The

Fig 9: Rhomboid version of the woven Log Cabin block on the mummy of a child. (©The Trustees of the National Museums of Scotland)

unknown child, for example, has a gilded mask and toenails, also breasts. Another mummy of a male in the collection of the British Museum has a different version of the rhomboid pattern, but only on the lower arms. In this instance there are no ornamental studs and the rhomboid shape starts with an off-centre square in one angle (4).

Square versions of the pattern can be found in animal mummies of the same period. Votive animal mummies were given as gifts to the gods and all species of animal were embalmed, from cows to falcons and even scorpions and crocodiles. Among the cat mummies in the British Museum is one with a recognisable Log Cabin pattern as we now know it – including the use of two colours, light and dark. (Fig 10) Another pattern variation in the same museum can be found in a mummified calf from Thebes. In this woven construction, the pattern that emerges is what is commonly called a key or meander pattern (5).

The use of coloured bandaging to wrap mummies in the Roman period is of particular interest since it also makes a connection with the tradition of using red in the centre of a Log Cabin block. Recycled household linen and clothing was the main source of bandaging in the mummification process; the strips were pasted with a resin mixed with sawdust, and the resin when dried formed a tough encasement. Only royal personages would have qualified for the best quality new linen. The colour of the dyed bandages would most probably have been a deep pink, the dye having come from the saff flower (Carthamus tinctorius L). Egyptologist John H. Taylor of the British Museum says: 'The use of a reddish pink – a solar colour – may have conveyed the notion of resurrection by the life-giving rays of the sun.'(6) Time and exposure to air have of course altered the colour of these original strips of linen. Instead of bright pink and white, what we see today is brown and beige. But the curiosity of pattern usage remains. In the woven version, we also have the practice of using light and dark sides to a square (pink and white) just as in traditional sewn Log Cabin blocks.

Weaving, whether to make baskets, mats or cloth, is an ancient craft that also bears examination in relation to a study of the Log Cabin pattern. Eva Wilson, who has published several design source books for the British Museum, refers to the paintings on the walls and ceiling of Egyptian tombs as a reflection of the woven mats that originally lined the tombs. Of particular note is a herringbone-style pattern where one arm of the pattern is a rectangle, and the other a rectangle composed of three strips. It dates from the second millennium BC. Other painted ceiling designs include squares within squares and key patterns. (7) Whether the weaving influence also extended to the design of the mummy wrappings is speculative: one theory is that the god Osiris, the god of death, influenced the use of design in the wrappings since remaining visuals of him demonstrate that he wore patterned clothing.

The relationship between weaving patterns and patchwork patterns and the influence of one on the other would make an excellent research project. One can easily see how the herringbone weave may have influenced the quilt border and the English quilt on page 37. The crossover of terminology that continues to the current day lends further weight to the relationship of the two textile mediums. Contemporary weavers give the name 'Log Cabin' to checkerboard weaves which quilters call Rail Fence but no one seems able to say how long the term has been in usage. British weaver Ann Sutton explains that the squares 'change step' by a deliberate mistake in the warp only. The use of one colour and then another, she says, is 'known as 'end-and-end' (warp) and 'pick-and-pick' (weft). (8)

In *The Key to Weaving published* in 1949, Mary E. Black referred to the Log Cabin weave as 'an old-time pattern', suggesting it could be used in either traditional or modern interiors

where a simple geometric pattern was desired (9). She recommended that it be used in upholstery, pillow covers, table scarves or runners, place mats, bags, purses and drapes. There are other examples of similarities in names between weaving and patchwork. Black, who published the book after retiring as Director of Handcrafts of the Province of Nova Scotia, founded the Canadian Guild of Weavers and was also honoured for her significant contribution to crafts. Another book on hand-weaving (10), by Mary Meigs Atwater, attributes American weaving to many of the old forms taken to the United States by the early colonists, in particular the Dutch who settled in New Amsterdam; the Mennonites of Pennsylvania; the Scots who settled in the southern uplands; the Irish who went to New Hampshire and the English Puritans of New England. The same usage for pattern names – like Log Cabin, Orange Peel, Blazing Star and Rose of Sharon – could indicate the early dual role of the homemaker as both weaver and quiltmaker, though probably an explanation of the cross influence is more complex.

A more specific relationship between weaving and, in this case, applied work, was documented in the Ohio quilt project where a direct influence was seen between the pineapple and grape vine motifs of a Jacquard coverlet woven for German customers by Edward W. Marshall and the intricate appliqué quilt made by his wife, Julia, in 1860 (11)

Fig 10: The light and dark shading of the cat mummy indicates the probable use of saff flower dye.
(© Copyright The Trustees of the British Museum)

Geometrics and the Greco-Roman Influence

Even before Log Cabin appeared as a woven pattern in Egypt, however, there were other influences at work – namely, the geometric patterns which began evolving in Greek art between 1100 and 700BC. Early painted pottery and small-scale sculpture show that simple geometrics were used: the more sophisticated geometric mosaics followed as a result of contact with Eastern cultures through trading. 'Between 725 and 650BC, Greek art absorbed a host of Oriental motifs and ideas and was profoundly transformed in the process,' states art historian H.W. Janson (12)

The Greeks first developed mosaic art as a pebble technique during their Classical and Hellenistic phases – about the last four centuries BC. The art of tesserae came later and is harder to attribute, though it is believed to have evolved in the eastern Mediterranean. We have the remains of the Roman seaside resort of Pompeii (destroyed by the eruption of Vesuvius in AD 79) as a reminder, however, of the early usage of geometrics in art. The box or cube, today known in patchwork as Tumbling Blocks, was first recorded in Pompeii, appearing at a time when the was especial interest in creating three-dimensional effects. Other associated forms, namely the meander, labyrinth and key patterns, appeared even earlier in the sixth millennium BC in Turkey and as pottery decoration in neolithic Europe. The key in itself is an interesting legacy. It is easily executed in the Log Cabin technique and historically it has appeared in the decorative designs of many different cultures.

The growth and influence of Rome meant an absorption and dissemination of other cultural influences, not only from Greece and other Mediterranean countries but also across southern Europe. Rome was dominant in the Mediterranean by 133 BC: by 43AD it had conquered as far west as Britain. Extant ancient mosaics are a vivid indicator of how geometric pattern travelled with the Roman conquerors. To get a feel for the variety of forms used in Roman pavements, one has only to consult *The Grammar of Ornament* written by Owen Jones in 1856 at a time of the revival of classical art forms. The Jones book is especially significant taken in the context of the period and coming as it did after the Great Exhibition of 1851 in London when the return to classical design was so overpowering. One has to ask, since most extant Log Cabin quilts date from about this period, what effect the classical revival, together with the increased availability of printed patterns, had on the design in relation to patchwork? We know that it appeared in other craft forms prior to the mid-19th century. And, we believe, with some confidence, that the use of the design in patchwork dates far earlier. Certainly, the classical revival was a strong influence in popularising geometric forms: the Jones book together with subsequent influential works like *Meyer's Ornament*, by Franz Sales Meyer, first published in Leipzig as *Ornamentale Formenlehre* in 1886, were welcomed inspiration for craftspeople working across different disciplines. The best example of the impact of mosaic design on patchwork sewing is found in Jones' pastiche of a Roman pavement:

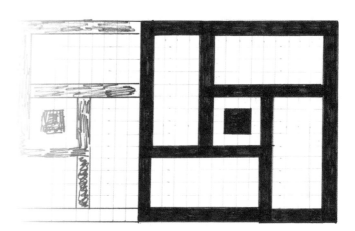

Fig 11: The mock mosaic floor drawn by Owen Jones in 1856 included this 'relative' of the Log Cabin block. It can still be seen in Roman excavations. (The Grammar of Ornament)

'...we have gathered together all the forms of mosaic pavement, which was such a feature in every home of the Romans, wherever their dominion extended. In the attempt at relief shown in several of the examples, we have evidence that their taste was no longer so refined as that of their Greek teachers. The borders, formed by a repetition of hexagons at the top and the sides of the page, are the types from which we may directly trace all that immense variety of Byzantine, Arabian and Moresque mosaics.'(13)

The Roman mosaic compendium produced by Jones did not include the box or cube pattern but it did show examples of three-dimensional meander designs, which he referred to as 'the attempt at relief', squares on point, mazes, chains, hexagons infilled with stars, triangles on point (Flying Geese), scrolls, squares within squares and yes, an early 'relative' of what we call the Log Cabin pattern (Fig 11). Evidence of this rendition still exists: the floor of a bedroom in Hadrian's Villa at Tivoli near Rome is one example; another is the Fishbourne Roman Palace near Chichester in England, where the pattern is used as both an edging and to cover an entire floor (14). Jones' *Grammar* certainly influenced Victorian needlewomen: mosaic patterns, often executed in fine velvets and silk, became a distinctive characteristic of needlework in the second half of the 19th century. Instead of the worn wools and recycled clothing of the utility quilt, which had often gone before, Log Cabin also acquired a genteel status and moved to the front parlour.

By Land and Sea: the Movement of Pattern

Mosaic art was just one of the cultural influences that the Romans took west across Europe. They spread their own culture in engineering, architecture, agriculture, coinage, banking and language. They were, however, not the only carriers of pattern and design. One has also to consider the early development of sea and trade routes and the exposure of one country to the culture of another. The Vikings are an example. Perhaps the most adventurous of the early seaborne navigators, the Vikings, from 900 AD, traded from Newfoundland in the west to Uzbekistan in the east, from Greenland in the north to the Mediterranean in the south. Archaeological finds on display in Jorvik, the Viking centre in York, England, attest to this far reach: on show is amber from the Baltic; sharpening stones from Shetland and Norway; a silk cap from the East; coins from Samarkand; cowrie shells from the Red Sea; stones, pottery and a brooch from the Rhineland; pins, a dress and cloak from Ireland.

These Scandinavian raiders and expeditionary scouts were essentially a pagan culture that had developed from the early Iron Age – a culture devoted to agriculture, hunting and trapping. Thus, their initial pirate forays into new territory were generally followed by farming settlers. Danish Vikings stormed York's Roman fortress in 866AD but it was Norwegian Vikings who had earlier raided the Scottish coasts from about 790AD. Orkney and Shetland were only two days' sail from the Norwegian coast and came under Viking rule in the 9th century. The islands remained in the possession of Norway until 1472: in that year they became part of Scotland as part of a royal marriage dowry. On their journeys along the west coast of Britain, the Vikings also stopped on the Isle of Man and Dublin before continuing north to the Faeroe Islands and Iceland. They reached Dublin, Ireland in 840AD, the same year it is believed they first entered the Mediterranean through the Straits of Gibraltar. By the 12th century, according to Thor Heyerdahl, it was 'so common for Vikings to visit the Mediterranean that the Norwegian King Sigurd Magnusson, while entering Gibraltar with sixty ships, had to fight another hostile Viking fleet on the way out.'(15) Although the Romans never occupied Scandinavia, their influence reached Northern Europe through the sea trade of the Vikings, who became an important conduit between the Mediterranean and countries to the west. In addition, after adopting Christianity, successive Norwegian kings made pilgrimages to Rome, while Leif Ericsson introduced Christianity into Greenland in 1000 AD.

Knowledge of early conquests and the development of trade routes makes for interesting speculation, especially when discussing the movement between cultures of repeat geometric patterns. Recent textile research has shown that there is a legacy of the Log Cabin pattern being used in Scandinavian countries - especially in

Fig 12: Drawing of the off-centre Log Cabin block that appears in the mosaic chapel of Lima Cathedral. The Cathedral was originally built in 1555 but has been rebuilt many times since following natural disasters.

Similarities and Differences – Europe

One is apt to make broad generalisations about the tradition of European quiltmaking. England, for example, will forever be associated with hexagons on papers and wholecloth quilts; France with boutis (padded quilting); and Holland with Indian chintz. It is hard to make any similar comments on style about quilts made in Germany because relatively few historic quilts have yet come to light. The book by the German author Schnuppe von Gwinner (16) does, however, show some spectacular examples of very complex applied work: in particular, one hanging with stars, soldiers, miners, Turks, hunters and various border geometrics including squares within squares and cables in the City Museum in Bautzen dating from 1776 to 1779; and leather patchwork pillows (used as church kneelers) with stars, flowers and nine-patch blocks from the 18th and 19th centuries from the Museum fur Kunst und Gewerbe, Hamburg. Outwith Germany, examples of early German quiltmaking also exist. The National Museums of Scotland hold an elaborate blue silk embroidered and quilted (in a grid) bed cover with coats of arms of the von Mansbach and von Budtlar families dated 1738. And, as an example of cross-country influence, the British quilt documentation project recorded a Crazy and Tumbling Blocks table cover of Austro-Prussian velvets made by a young British bride who had gone to Germany in the 1840s (17). Then there is the pieced, applied and embroidered Bohemian bedcover from the Austro-Hungarian Empire in the Victoria and Albert Museum in London, dated 1796. As 18th and 19th century immigrants to North America, the Germans became prolific quiltmakers and a number of academic studies have sought to place or explain the German contribution to quiltmaking. Certainly, as the Ohio quilt study demonstrated, the legacy of appliqué from the old country is one that flourished in the new world.

Sweden and Norway. It was also popular in Scotland, Ireland and the Isle of Man – all places connected with the Vikings and their expeditionary routes. It is a curious coincidence. Perhaps the Log Cabin pattern, like so many other geometric patterns, travelled overland or by sea from Greece and Egypt to Europe and hence to the new world. Perhaps the Spanish explorers and conquistadors, in their ventures to America, Mexico, Peru and Chile, had a role to play in transporting geometric design. Spain too was once a province of Rome and certainly the decorative tile influence travelled. Blue and yellow tiles shipped from Spain in 1620 to decorate the walls of the Franciscan monastery in Lima are one example. And then, there is the mosaic chapel in memory of Francisco Pizarro (1471-1541) in the Cathedral on Lima's main square: its extensive tile work includes many designs, one of which is the off-centre Log Cabin square, partially decorated in gold. (Fig 12)

Spain and Italy, the warmer countries of Europe, have yet to divulge any strong patchwork legacy. There is, however, evidence of remarkable early wholecloth quilts: one from Italy with a mid-16th century Mediterranean galley, stitched in gold silk is cited by Avril Colby in *Quilting* (London, 1972). Colby also mentions early Indo-Portuguese quilts with animals, birds, human figures and geometric patterns. Such a quilt, from the early 17th century, was recorded in the British quilt documentation programme. Made of silk, its stuffed quilting patterns included hunting scenes.

The legacy of quilted clothing, for both military and domestic use, is common to most European countries. But the patchwork tradition would seem to have flourished more in those countries where warm bedding was a need. On the Baltic, for example, quiltmaking is carried on in Estonia by a flourishing workshop (Lapitood Tilkkutyo) in the centre of Tallinn run by Anni Kreem and Ene Pars. The word quilt in Estonian is Lapitekk (patch-blanket) and the Log Cabin pattern is highly favoured in the many different household items made in this unusual studio. (Fig 13) When you ask Anni why, you are told that around 1900 it was a favourite of her grandmother and that her grandmother was a tailoress who worked in a manor owned by a Baltic German nobleman in southern Estonia. At the time, Estonia was part of the Russian empire but the Baltic provinces were culturally shaped by the descendants of the 13th century German crusaders. Patchwork was also popular at the time, according to Anni, on the western coast of Estonia, probably because of the Swedish minority living there.

The work of recording historic quilts on mainland Europe is ongoing and generally in its infancy. Britain remains the only European country to have undertaken a full-blown documentation programme, recording more than 4,000 items over a three-year period and that programme excluded Ireland. Holland, which has a prolific quilt ('Doorgestikte Deken') heritage, has benefited from the research carried out by An Moonen - first on the collection of the Netherlands Open Air Museum in Arnhem (18), where she was textile curator until 1992, and latterly for the book 'T Is Al Beddegoet (It is all Bedware) (uitgeverij Terra Zutphen, 1996). The Log Cabin pattern, says An, is 'rare' in Holland and she knows of only four such quilts, dating between 1850 and 1860. Two are in the Arnhem Collection. One is woollen, in a Barn Raising layout with red centres in the blocks; the other is a mix of wool, silk and cotton. It has a Light and Dark layout and is also made with red centres. A third Log Cabin quilt, from the same period, is in the Religious Museum at Uden and was made by nuns

in the closed cloister of Soeterbeek near Deursen/Ravenstein. Made of silk, wool, velvet and cotton, the blocks have black centres and the quilt has no recognisable layout. In An's opinion, possible 'influence from the US seems out of the question', in terms of patterns crossing the Atlantic, since all three quilts mentioned come from poor areas, which were farmed by peasants who had little communication with the outside world. There was trade with Sweden at the time – another possible connection – but not in the relevant areas where the quilts were made. Interestingly, the Log Cabin pattern was used as a needlework stitch in Berlin wool samplers in Holland from about 1840 to 1890: samples are in the collection at Arnhem.

Extant Log Cabin quilts made prior to 1850 are rare, but then so too is the survival rate of other patchworks from the same period. Even more rare (almost non-existent) is the signed and dated Log Cabin quilt. To a great degree one has to look at

Fig 13: Estonia's thriving quilt workshop (Lapitood Tilkkutyo) where the Log Cabin pattern is a favourite.

existing museum collections or the work of quilt researchers to 'get a feel' for a country's traditions. Certainly the work of quilt historian Joan Foster, working under the auspices of the Norwegian Quilt Association (19), points to the popularity of the Log Cabin pattern in that country. In a survey of quilts undertaken in Norway, she recorded 57 Log Cabin quilts out of a total of 202 items. Of this number, 44 were made in Norway by Norwegians, nine were 'probably' made in Norway, three were made in the United States (two by Norwegian immigrants) and one was made in Denmark. The oldest Log Cabin quilt, made between 1850 and 1870, was made of wool in a Barn Raising layout and was used as a sleigh cover by a local doctor some time during his tenure in Orkdalen between 1846 and 1888. The sewing technique is unusual in that it combines two methods: the red centre square is surrounded by folded strips of wool which have been overlapped and basted to the foundation, while the outer edges of the blocks are unfolded strips sewn to the backing. The technique of folding strips of fabric and sewing them in an overlapping manner is not uncommon in existing European quilts and was often used in Victorian pieces with luxury fabrics of velvet and silk. Working with wool in this technique, however, made the quilts very heavy: the doctor's quilt doubly so because it was also backed with a red and black woollen blanket.

The Norwegian quilts recorded show a variety of Log Cabin layouts - Barn Raising, stripes or Straight Furrows, Zig Zag, Cross, Light and Dark and Japanese Lanterns. Some individual blocks were crude in construction, perhaps with only two rounds of 'logs'; some were far better executed with, for example, embroidery in the centre square. The Pineapple, Courthouse Steps, and traditional blocks were all used and in addition, the survey turned up other strip quilts composed of blocks of strips (Rail Fence) and even a quilt of wools and suitings with Chevron blocks (strips sewn on the diagonal) laid in alternate rows to Pinwheel blocks.

In Denmark, where no official documentation programme has yet been undertaken and where few museums have quilts in their collections, quiltmaker Birgit Glüsing of Copenhagen has undertaken personal research of the country's tradition. To date she has compiled information on about 100 items. Most date from 1900, though one finely pieced work of wool triangles with a centre star was made prior to 1825. 'I don't think you can talk about a Danish patchwork tradition,' she comments, 'or about a favourite pattern. Most things found so far are very simple scrap quilts, although there are exceptions. I have found quite a number of Crazy quilts, some hexagons, a few stars and so on.'(20) Many of the Danish examples of patchwork examined by Birgit were pieced covers as opposed to layered quilts. 'Old Danish patchwork,' she says, 'is seldom quilted,' and in fact the Danes do not have a word for patchwork. The pieced covers would have been used over thick cotton wholecloth quilts or fillings for the summer: in winter the traditional Danish bedding was the much heavier eiderdown.

Generally the Log Cabin quilts discovered to date support Birgit's observation about the Danish quilts being simple in construction. Of particular interest is a quilt from Northern Jutland made by Maren Peterson Andersen who lived from 1868 to 1953. (See page 43) She was the wife of a smallholder and gave birth to 17 children. Despite the large family and her domestic and farming duties, however, she found time to make many quilts – including one for each of her children plus rugs or cushions for her grandchildren. This particular variation of a Log Cabin – with an outsize red centre and only two logs, turned on point and finished with large triangles, was made about 1930. Sewn on a linen foundation, the quilt was used by an elderly gentleman during his afternoon nap.

None of Maren Andersen's surviving children could tell where their mother got her ideas to make quilts. She did have cousins who emigrated to Iowa in 1892 and with whom she kept in contact and who sent her fabric. But Northern Jutland has also been found to have many examples of early patchwork so the influence was more likely local. Fabrics used were often recycled from clothing and Maren Andersen's comforter is filled with tweed and backed with coarse, loosely woven brown linen that has been folded over the top to create an edge.

Statistical information has not yet been compiled in Sweden, but the Log Cabin tradition is strong. Historian and collector Asa Wettre describes it as 'the most common design.'(21) The Block House ('block hus') or Stock House ('stock hus') as it is called, has been sewn in Sweden in all its variations from traditional to Courthouse Steps to Pineapple. One of the more unusual variations, which Asa calls 'Grandmother's Quilt' (Mormor's quilt) can be seen on page 91. The name was supplied to her following publication of her book in English in the United States in 1995. A letter from an American family of Swedish descent informed Asa the pattern was carried by their ancestors to the United States. With

Fig 14: Wide borders and heavy wadding typify the
Swedish approach to this Log Cabin Cross. Made by
Alma Johansson in the 1920s. 120 x 240cm (47 x 94in).
(Collection of Asa Wettre)

Swedish quilts, one can also see the use of strips to make Rail Fence patterns and even the chevron strip as shown on page 73.

Asa's own quilt collection, which tours under the title *Lapptacken – en kulturskatt* (Patchwork quilts – a Treasure of Culture) has been seen in more than 30 European venues since 1989. Together with her book, *Old Swedish Quilts*, it shows ample evidence of the Swedish Log Cabin tradition – its similarities and differences. There is a 'sister' of the unusual Danish quilt made by Maren Andersen, where the squares are turned on point and finished with triangles: the difference is that the Swedish quilt is more even in its colour placement, and individual blocks have black centres surrounded by a red strip as opposed to Andersen's more naive use of a red centre surrounded by different colours. Both were made about the same time. Assembly of individual blocks generally follows the Light and Dark tradition but variations can be seen in the centre square, which can be quite large, often dark, and sometimes pieced as two or four triangles, or, in one more interesting version, as four squares surrounded by strips. Layouts are similar – Furrows, Light and Dark (also called Sunshine and Shadow), with one of the older quilts, a wedding quilt dating from the 1880s, showing a framed diamond layout.

Sweden, like Germany, also has a long tradition of unusual patchwork cushions. In Sweden, however, the cushions, which date from the middle of the 18th century, were used specifically within the wedding ceremony. Generally pieced in triangles, squares and rectangles - sometimes with a star centre - their interest lies in the use of covered cord as an outlining between individual self-coloured shapes. What makes some of the Swedish Log Cabin quilts look different to the outsider's eye (apart from the small details mentioned above) is the use of very thick wadding and sometimes very wide quilted borders in simple zig zag or diagonal lines. The extra heavy wadding was obviously a necessity in the cold Swedish winters. And, the wide self-coloured borders are a very effective frame to the patchwork as witness the quilt made by Alma Johansson in the 1920s. (Fig 14) Patchwork other than Log Cabin was also used in this type of quilt. The Wettre book, for example, shows two red quilts with square on point medallions from the 1930s, made by Berta Larsson. These two examples are very reminiscent of the commercially made 'Comfy' quilts documented in the British quilt documentation project from about the same period. In the latter instance, one plain fabric and one print fabric were sandwiched together and machine quilted. Then a diamond was cut from the centre, reversed and set in, giving a self-coloured quilt with a print medallion centre (22).

The British Isles

Moving from Sweden and Norway, crossing the North Sea to the British Isles, one finds other strong quiltmaking traditions. Scotland, Ireland and the Isle of Man are most closely associated with the Log Cabin pattern. When the British quilt documentation project undertook its survey between 1990 and 1993 (which did not include Ireland) it recorded quilts in private ownership from various parts of the country. As anticipated, the most popular pieced pattern was the hexagon (587 items in total). This was followed by quilts that had squares as the predominant pattern (439). The number of Log Cabin quilts recorded was 217. They were documented in a wide variety of fabrics and layout and included Pineapple and Courthouse Steps variations and even logs set around a hexagon. One of the most unusual layouts discovered was sewn about 1900 in Cornwall. Made of plain coloured fabrics, it looks like squares on point set in frames (23).

Although there are no large museum collections of quilts within Scotland, many of the smaller museums reflect the popularity of the pattern. Collectors too have found Scotland fertile ground for Log Cabin quilts, though the supply of 19th century examples has become less abundant. Scottish Log Cabin quilts do not have a particular characteristic unless one points to the frequent appearance of Turkey Red prints in the composition (see page 8). Given that Glasgow was a thriving centre for the production and export of Turkey Red cloth, from the late 18th century until the early 20th century, this is to be expected. Scottish Log Cabin quilts made in the latter part of the 19th century display all manner of techniques, layout and fabric. For a country where knitting and weaving were strong traditional textile crafts, it is not difficult to find the occasional woollen quilt – or, more rarely, the quilt made with tartan. One example in the collection of the Perth

Museum & Art Gallery, made with ties, tartan and miscellaneous fabrics, shows how dynamic such use of fabric can be in a traditional pattern. (See cover and page 61) This quilt, which has almost a modern feel, and another, both executed in a Light and Dark format, came to the Museum in 1942. They were described in the accession list as 'two quilts made from squares formed from strips of cloth with printed linen backs'. Both are early – circa 1860 - 1870 – and completely hand sewn in traditional manner to a foundation with red centres. One speculates that the donor in 1942, a Miss Margaret Morgan, from the small Fife village of Newburgh, was getting her affairs in order by dispersing her treasures. She died at the end of the War.

The sewing techniques in old Scottish Log Cabin quilts vary from folded overlapping strips to the more traditional stitch and flip. Block centres vary in size and colour and in some cases are non-existent. The blue and white Ayrshire quilt on page 79, for example, contains a number of blocks where the foundation becomes the centre square, surrounded by folded strips. As in every other country where the Log Cabin pattern was popular, surviving quilts demonstrate a divergence between the more roughly sewn utilitarian examples and the finer, more luxurious items. The simple Log Cabin quilt that covers the small box bed in a cottage at the Auchindrain Township Open Air Museum, near Inveraray on the West Coast, gives the authentic in situ picture of quilts past – and how a colourful piece of patchwork would have enlivened an otherwise dull interior. The box bed itself often dictated another practice – that of edging with lace the side of the quilt that hung over the front of the bed.

Use of embellishment and pieced work in the borders is a special feature of the Log Cabin quilts in the collection of the Ceres Folk Museum in Fife. One red and white cross quilt has an especially fine scalloped red border with embroidery, believed to date from the latter part of the 19th century (see page 116). Another very fine Log Cabin quilt made in the Courthouse Steps manner, with pink and white prints alternating with dark grey/black/brown and some tartan prints (each block boasting a dominant large red wool centre) can also be found in the Ceres collection. It is the border that interests. On the two longest sides, it has a pieced herringbone pattern and a Turkey Red strip edged with crochet (see page 118). Dated between 1850 and 1860, it comes from an estate near Cupar in Fife. Of equal

interest in the sphere of unusual Log Cabin borders is the milliner's quilt in the collection of the Angus Folk Museum in Glamis Village, near Glamis Castle, the family home of the Earls of Strathmore and a royal residence since 1372. It was the childhood home of her late Majesty, Queen Elizabeth the Queen Mother. The rich fabrics from the milliner's shop – ribbons, velvets, brocades, lace trims and silks have been used to make the blocks, in a Light and Dark layout, and also to form triangular points for the border (see page 117) The quilt has a large octagonal medallion with a dark red plush centre which has been made in the Log Cabin style: all strips in the quilt are folded and stitched to a backing in overlapping rows including the medallion centre. The quilt was made in a Forfar shop run by Miss Jane Yeaman about 1860 or 1870. The Museum's other quilt of interest is made from cottons with quite large red centres. The dark prints, which include Paisley prints, dominate the cross layout. Purchased by the founder of the Museum, the late Lady Jean Maitland, a patchworker herself, this quilt is said to date from 1878.

Moving north in Scotland, one stops briefly in the Orkney Isles, which with Shetland, Caithness, Sutherland and the Western Isles, were once Viking colonies. Orkney today retains much of the Scandinavian influence – including place and family names and a rich tradition of Norse legends and folklore. There is archaeological evidence of flax crops, spinning and weaving, and Viking design influences remain to this day in items such as jewellery. The Vikings worked in metal to a high standard, and also excelled in carving: their ancient alphabet (runes) in stone can be seen in Maes Howe in Orkney, an ancient burial chamber.

Present day quiltmakers on Orkney, who can recall the work of previous generations, talk of utilitarian and simple pieced tops, or recycled sugar or flour bags tacked onto worn blankets. 'Twilts', as they were called, were functional and economical and the cotton covering on the blankets was stitched by hand with just enough needlework to hold the covering in place. It was the blanket that was important and wool from the annual shearing on the islands was often sent to the mainland to be spun or woven into blankets. Initially, the abundant local supply of wool gave Orkney a strong knitting tradition and, at one time, the raw wool to weave 'wadmel', a black cloth for clothing. Linen was woven in Orkney well into the 18th century, but was later replaced by cheaper printed fabrics from the mainland. And yes, the occasional old Log Cabin quilt can be found on the island, but only in private ownership.

Another island in British waters that fostered a quilt culture was the Isle of Man, off the west coast of the mainland between England and Ireland. Here Log Cabin is called the Roof pattern. The Isle of Man has strong connections with Cleveland, Ohio, to which many people from the island emigrated. Indeed, a Log Cabin quilt in the Manx Museum collection is known to have been made between 1870 and 1880 in the United States (24) by Mrs John Benjamin Cowley (nee Killey).

Contemporary quiltmakers on the Isle of Man lay claim to the Log Cabin pattern as being 'the true Manx pattern' but not enough examples survive to give any idea of layout or colour preferences, and if one asks where the pattern might have come from, there is the enigmatic reply 'Look to the sea'. What makes the Manx Log Cabin of particular interest is the method of construction, which has been handed down and which still causes great interest and a challenge to contemporary needlewomen (see page 110). Its main feature is the tuck or pleat. Given that nowadays everyone who wants to make a quilt is blessed with an infinite number of tools and a variety of fabrics, it is hard to envisage

quiltmaking ancestors working by the light of a candle, with only a knife or their teeth as cutting implements; worn clothing as fabric; and finger and hand measurements in place of a ruler or tape measure. The traditional technique is ably demonstrated to this day by Joan Thrussell in the Cregneash Village Folk Museum – a museum associated with 19th century farming life.

Ireland, with its distinctive tradition of red on white appliqué quilts and the 'wave' quilting pattern, also counts Log Cabin among its many pieced quilts. The Ulster Folk and Transport Museum at Cultra, Holywood in Northern Ireland has the largest quilt collection in the British Isles, numbering some 500 items. The Log Cabin pattern accounts for about eight per cent of the total while the most popular pattern is the strippy quilt (part of the wholecloth quilt family) followed by variations of the nine-patch (including Irish Chain), baskets, stars, diamonds or hexagons, perhaps indicating the English legacy.

In Ireland, the sewing of patchwork was included within needlework instruction in the school system. From 1814, the Kildare Place Society, which trained teachers, included needlework in its curriculum and in 1853 its

Fig 15: Detail of a heavy quilt from Northern Ireland made of velvet, hand-woven tweed, wool and red flannel backed by hessian. It demonstrates yet another variation on placing strips around a square. 163 x 192cm (64 x 77in). (©National Museum and Galleries of Northern Ireland, Ulster Folk & Transport Museum)

needlework manual included instructions for sewing template (especially hexagon) patchwork (25), but not specifically the Log Cabin pattern. Like Scotland, Ireland was a textile-producing country – cotton, linen and wool – and the two countries traded with each other, which probably explains the common use of Turkey Red. Some of the most interesting quilts were made from fabrics from this textile manufacture or by people who worked in allied occupations. Thus you find examples of wool from tailors' sample books and cotton off-cuts from shirt-making factories, or quilts backed with linen. Damask, another Irish-produced fabric, can also appear in pieced work. The more prized silks, satins and ribbons, which came from outwith the country, were also saved and used by milliners and dressmakers for more elaborate works. Many of the existing quilts made with shirting fabrics date from the 1920s and 1930s, though the industry itself dates from the 1830s. By 1845, there were hundreds of weavers and shirt makers employed in Derry and the industry grew even larger some years later when the sewing machine became available. By the 1880s, Derry was producing over three million shirts a year, using both outworkers and factory employees. Glasgow too had a shirt making tradition during the same period and if one should happen across a blue and white Log Cabin quilt, either in Ireland or in Scotland, then the fabrics can usually be attributed to the shirt factory source (see page 79).

Log Cabin quilts in the Ulster Folk Museum collection include some unusual patterns. Techniques are traditional (sewn to a foundation) and there are a few examples of folded over-lapping strips. A Rail Fence quilt made prior to 1890, boasting a red frill, uses this technique. Only one quilt in the entire collection follows the Courthouse Steps mode. The Pineapple variation has been used in both Scotland and Ireland, with the latter having one red and white version which the owners called 'Soldier's Wreath' – perhaps a reference to the traditional red poppy wreaths used to honour war dead, a practice which began at the end of World War I. Curiously, while some quilts in the Manx Museum on the Isle of Man can be said to demonstrate an Irish influence, the unusual Manx method of sewing Log Cabin blocks did not travel to Ireland, Scotland, Wales or even England: it remains unique.

Perhaps the most unusual Log Cabin quilt in the Irish collection falls within the 'Tile' category – but with a difference (Fig 15). The large dark 6 cm centre is surrounded by six very narrow folded rows of logs and finished off with a 3 cm strip that is roughly quilted in a zig zag pattern. Hand-woven tweeds, velvets and wool are among the fabrics used and the blocks are put together with red flannel sashing. It is backed with hessian, making it a very heavy quilt.

The Migrants

The many European nationalities that settled North America had an influence on quiltmaking that is hard to disentangle in terms of attributing ethnicity. Armed with sewing skills, and needlework tools, sometimes even quilted clothing and bedding, the early settlers also carried cultural influences that cross-fertilised in the new land.

Utilitarian quilts were made in abundance on the new frontiers just as they had been in Europe. One is especially reminded of early 'Hit and Miss" quiltmaking in Canada, sometimes from handwoven wools (26) or the late 19th century Wagga rugs made in Australia by men who used twine to stitch wheat bags as covers when camping outdoors. (In the hands of women, the Wagga became a cheap cotton or cretonne cover housing a recycled filling of worn clothing.) (27). But, overall, the development of the quilt was a more complex journey. The wealthier European immigrants, bringing a legacy of fine embroidery, broderie perse, lace making and other artistic textile pursuits made one kind of contribution to quiltmaking: the less affluent immigrants, trying simply to keep body and soul together, made another. As new colonies and republics developed, and economic necessities merged with a potent desire for artistic expression, the patchwork quilt became a blend of inherited cultural influences.

European settlers who developed the new countries carried both physical and mental 'baggage'. In addition to utilitarian household items like bedding, for example, most immigrants would probably have packed some kind of keepsake from the 'old country'. More than likely it had some form of decoration or pattern: perhaps a Welsh love spoon carved with hearts and flowers; or a treasured book of German lithographs with an embellished frontispiece; or, from Sweden, an embroidered apron. The ornamental use of pattern on objects has been known since antiquity and even the poorest of families would have had objects that were decorated. And, if they did not have a physical object to stimulate recall, then certainly there were memories.

Chambers 20th Century Dictionary defines memory as 'the power of retaining and reproducing mental or sensory impressions.' In writing about the dynamics of visual form, Maurice de Sausmarez expanded the definition: 'Every visual experience is at one and the same time a receiving of fragmentary information, a giving of form to these visual sensations and the arousing of felt response.'(28) For immigrants from rural environments, the memories would have been simple and related to their farming experiences: thus today one can easily make the visual connection between the most elementary strips in a crofter's tilled field of the late 17th century, with a form of weaving which directly imitated that image and a form of patchwork called Rail Fence. (Fig16) The farming relationship with the Log Cabin pattern cannot be denied – even the traditional names given to layouts signal the influence.

Australia and Canada, the two Commonwealth countries which experienced large influxes of settlers from the British Isles, both have quilt traditions, but with a difference. Canada, the more prolific in terms of output of quilts, had a harsher climate and more immigrants. Australia too had cold winters, but their inclination towards sheep farming inevitably directed them towards woollen blankets. America had both the need for quilts because of cold winters and greater numbers of potential quiltmakers. The vast differences in growth of population also had a bearing on quiltmaking activity. In 1850, Australia had only a population of 400,000 (the figure increasing dramatically to one million in the next ten years due to the gold rushes). This compared with almost 2.5 million in Canada and over 23 million in the United States.

Quilts often travelled with the settlers and some records have survived. Mary Conroy in her book *300 Years of Canada's Quilts* refers to the great-grandmother of one Fred Keenan of Latchford, Ontario who brought from Ireland in the mid-1800s 'a sturdy, warm, practical, yet still colourful Log Cabin quilt'. (29). In Australia one can also find similar examples of 'travelling' quilts: an early Log Cabin quilt from the same period (circa 1850-70) of silk grosgrain ribbon and black velvet (30) transported from Cornwall, and a Queen Victoria Jubilee Log Cabin quilt made in England in 1887 (31). The latter, another rich confection of silks, featuring a Light and Dark layout in the border and Courthouse Steps blocks in the middle, has four embroidered panels with the shamrock, thistle, leek and rose and a centre Rail Fence block made up of Jubilee ribbons. What has yet to be discovered (if ever) is a Log

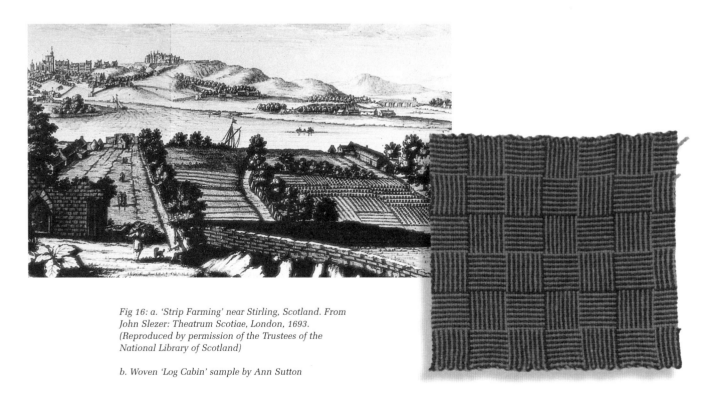

Fig 16: a. 'Strip Farming' near Stirling, Scotland. From John Slezer: Theatrum Scotiae, London, 1693. (Reproduced by permission of the Trustees of the National Library of Scotland)

b. Woven 'Log Cabin' sample by Ann Sutton

Cabin quilt made aboard one of the convict ships sailing from England to 'Van Diemen's Land' in the first half of the 19th century. Thousands of women were transported and countless quilts made aboard ships through the influence and help of the Quaker reformer, Elizabeth Fry. Only one such quilt bearing a date (June 1841) and inscription has been found, however, and it is a frame quilt with appliqué, piecing and broderie perse (32) now in the collection of the National Gallery of Australia in Canberra.

It is generally acknowledged that the English/Irish patchwork tradition of the 19th century influenced quiltmaking in Australia. In 1861, the number of people living in Australia who could claim Britain as their birthplace was over 630,000 of whom almost 177,500 were from Ireland and over 97,000 from England (not all British countries of origin were recorded).

Australia, North America and the British Isles all shared the late 19th century enthusiasm for the Log Cabin quilt. The pattern, as cited earlier, seemed particularly popular with luxury fabrics and quilts made for 'show'. Irish immigrant Jeannette Dick from Belfast made her trousseau quilt from the leftover silks and satins in the drapery shop where she worked in South Melbourne (33) about 1867 – a Courthouse Steps variation with 238 blocks and a ruffle edge. About the same time, some unknown maker was also using these finer fabrics to make a cushion cover using the European technique of overlapped folded strips stitched to a backing. (34) The latter example is on display in Patrick Taylor's Cottage, a folk museum in Albany, Western Australia.

Ribbons were an important inclusion in this penchant for the more luxurious Log Cabin quilts on both sides of the Atlantic – especially if printed

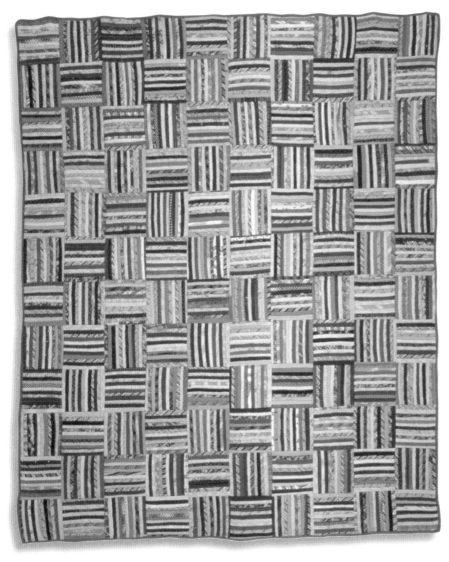

c. 19th century 'Fence Rail' quilt from Ontario. Mixed cotton and wool backed with home-dyed bags. Quilted in squares from the back. 155 x 180cm (60.5 x 70.5in) (© Canadian Museum of Civilization, catalogue no. 79-11, image no.S79-4124)

Fig 17: Branded silk tobacco ribbons, originally used to tie bunches of cigars, were meticulously sewn to a cotton foundation in this Pineapple quilt. c. 1900. 165 x 168cm (65 x 66in). (Courtesy of Michigan State University Museum)

with historical references – and they are a good marker for dating. With the British 'luxury' quilts, there was Queen Victoria and celebrations of her reign. In America, a quiltmaker might use a memorial ribbon to former American presidents, such as Ulysses S. Grant or James A. Garfield. The use of ribbons in quilts reached its zenith in the United States with the Tobacco Ribbon quilt. Printed silk ribbons, normally used to wrap bunches of cigars, were saved, laboriously stitched to a backing and sometimes embellished with embroidery, in the style of a crazy quilt. One of the finest examples of this practice can be found in the Pineapple-style quilt in the collection of Michigan

State University dated 1900 (Fig 17). In Britain, the tobacco 'silks' took another form – as textile 'cards' in cigarette packets. Printed with many different images – flowers, flags, footballers etc - they too became quiltmaker's collectables from about 1911 to the 1930s.

The popularity of the luxury Log Cabin quilt in the latter part of the 19th century also coincided with the increased domestic use of the sewing machine. Isaac Merritt Singer, who perfected the first practical sewing machine in Boston in 1850, made it possible for families of modest means to use this labour-saving device. But of course, he was not the first: various inventors in France, Germany,

England, Australia and the United States had either patented or been trying to manufacture sewing machines from 1755, when a German immigrant in London took out a patent for a needle to be used for mechanical sewing. Singer was, however, the one who successfully sold to the mass market both nationally and internationally: he opened his first European branch in Paris in 1855 and another a year later in Glasgow, Scotland. By 1863, he was also operating in Hamburg, Germany.

The sewing machine was a boon to quiltmakers everywhere and one of the earliest luxury Log Cabin quilts to be made with this new mechanical device was the quilt by Emily Genevieve Marks, believed to have been made about 1857, before her marriage to Joseph T. Clay, a distant relation of Henry Clay, a prominent Kentucky politician and presidential candidate. (Fig. 18) Made of silk and wool, it was also unusual in its design (for the period) – that of six-sided 'blocks' around a hexagon centre – executed in the Log Cabin technique. A quilt of wool, cotton and silk, sewn in the same manner, was also recorded in the British quilt documentation programme in Scotland. The provenance of this quilt, however, was not known and, judging from the fabrics, it appeared to have been made about 1900. It was hand sewn, the hexagon centres were blue and it had a red ruffle as a border.

The use of the Log Cabin pattern continued in Australia right through the first half of the 20th century. Prior to 1970 and the revival of patchwork and quilting, the Log Cabin pattern, along with Suffolk Puffs, crazy patchwork, medallion quilts, utility quilts, Wagga rugs, pieced-over-papers geometric shapes, and embroidered quilts remained the most used styles in Australia (35). From available evidence, some of the Log Cabin quilts in Australian collections do show, however, an individuality or departure from the British influence: in particular, the quilt by Nicholes Wallace on page 118, and a 20th century soldier's quilt. In addition to a most unusual border, the former quilt features the rare use of an off-centre block where the starting square is in one corner instead of the centre. The latter, made in Queensland in the 1940s, includes wool fabric from army uniforms and is tied and stuffed with an army blanket (36).

Whereas Australian quiltmaking before 1945 was largely influenced by immigrants from the British Isles and particularly England and Ireland, North America had more of an ethnic mix from Europe. Within this mix, however, some nationalities appear to have had a particularly strong influence. This is evidenced in those quilt documentation programmes by individual American states that have set their investigations in the context of ethnic history; the most interesting have also presented statistical information regarding the popularity of individual patterns. The results of the Rhode Island research, for example, reveal that the Log Cabin pattern was the most prolific pattern used, after crazy patchwork, between 1850 and 1899. Although ethnicity was not related to pattern in the statistics, it was interesting to note that out of the 280 cases where nationality could be reported, 80% of the quilts recorded were by English quiltmakers; only 10% by French Canadians and 5.7% by Irish. (37) Rhode Island, a state closely associated with textile manufacture, had an influx of Irish tenant farmers from the 1820s, followed by French Canadians after 1860, followed by British, Swedish and German settlers after the American Civil War, followed by skilled textile mechanics from England and Scotland.

In the study of Ohio's old quilts (38), a study which recorded 7,000 quilts over 53 'discovery days', two distinct ethnic-related traditions appear: the stylistic red and green floral appliqué quilts made by German settlers between 1850 and 1860; and pieced blocks, alternating with plain blocks set on point with two borders, from 1880 onwards. Made by German sectarians (Mennonites, Amish, Zoarites, Brethren) these quilts did not contain print fabrics but rather the solid colours used in sectarian clothing. Ohio is a state with a strong European mix: in addition to Germans, early settlers were Irish, English, Scots, Welsh, French and Swiss. The Irish and German labourers came to help with the construction of the Erie Canal (1825-32); the Welsh to work in the mines; the English to work in the pottery industry; and the Irish Catholics to work in manufacturing.

The Ohio study does deal with the Log Cabin pattern to some extent, pointing out that it was mentioned in print for a commendation at the Ohio State Fair in 1863. The earliest Log Cabin quilts recorded in the project, however, were from the late 1860s through the early 1870s, with the majority made between 1870 and 1895. Another point made by the study was the confusion of names: an album block pattern from *The Farm and Fireside* dated 15 March 1887 was titled 'Log Cabin'; a month later, the same block was being called 'Album' in the same publication.

The West Virginia project (39) discovered the

*Fig 18: Hexagonal Log Cabin quilt by Emily Genevieve
Marks, whose initials appear in the centre. Fabrics include
silk and wool. 1857. 191 x 204cm (71 x 79.5in) Photo by
Jim Roshan. (Kentucky Library and Museum, Western
Kentucky University, Bowling Green, Ky)*

pieced star was the most often used pattern (440 out of 3,898), with the crazy style next (421), followed by the hexagon flower garden (240). There were only 100 that fell within the Log Cabin category. Again, ethnicity was not related to pattern in the study, but the ancestry records noted that the top four nationalities allied to quiltmaking were English (530); German (352); Irish (303); and Scots (202). Leaving out the Welsh, who did not figure in the top four, the settlers from England, Ireland and Scotland totalled 1,035, accounting for almost one-third of the quilts recorded.

Widening the search to include string quilts also throws up another interesting find in *The Quilts of Tennessee, Images of Domestic Life Prior to 1930*. Although Log Cabin quilts were not included among the popularly used patterns (stars of one form or another took that accolade), the frequency of string quilts was considered important enough to be mentioned (40). Of the 1,050 pieced quilts recorded, 47 had been made by the string technique.

In Canada, the connection between British settlers and the Log Cabin pattern is particularly strong. In the late 1700s groups of French as well as German and English migrants resettling from the

United States began populating Canada. Large numbers of immigrants from the British Isles continued this settlement in the mid-1800s – a period which relates directly to early extant Log Cabin quilts. The Canadian census of 1870-71 recorded a total population of 3.6 million. The largest two groups within this statistic were the French (1 million) and the British (2.1 million). In a survey of quiltmaking on Prince Edward Island, Sherrie Davidson makes several observations regarding ethnic parentage of quilt patterns. One is particularly relevant:

'Throughout the past one hundred years, however, patterns chosen by Arcadian (French) quiltmakers were largely those preferred by Islanders whose ancestors originated in the British Isles. Log Cabin, Sawtooth, Dresden Plate and Star variations recur in largest measure in both populations.'(41)

Although the French settled Prince Edward Island in 1720, they comprised only one-eighth of the population, compared to three-quarters with British antecedents. The quiltmakers on Prince Edward Island shared in the Log Cabin 'trends' experienced in Australia, Britain and the United States – the penchant for using luxury fabrics such as silk, satin and taffeta in their quilts in the 1880s and 1890s – for both Log Cabin and crazy patterns. One quilt that was recorded featured a silk portrait of Queen Victoria, printed to commemorate her Golden Jubilee in 1887. Of particular interest in the survey was the first all-cotton Log Cabin quilt – 1907 – to be recorded in a Pineapple pattern, called by French quiltmakers Concombre or 'Cucumber'.

Other indicators also strengthen the British/Canadian/Log Cabin pattern relationship. Ruth McKendry, who spent years researching Canadian quilts and woven bedcoverings – talking to the quiltmakers and weavers and collecting the often discarded fruits of their labours – made this reply when asked if she could relate ethnic background to the Log Cabin pattern: 'Upon consideration I think it probable that Log Cabin quilts occur more often in areas settled by immigrants from the British Isles. I have seen one Log Cabin quilt made by a woman in the German area in Renfrew County whose family came from Germany.'(42).

The McKendry Collection of quilts, blankets and bedding is now part of The Canadian Museum of Civilization in Quebec In the foreword to her book, William E. Taylor, Jr, then Director of the Museum (when it was called The National Museum of Man) commented on 'the brutal, isolated struggle that English, Scots and Irish immigrants endured pioneering in Upper Canada,' adding further 'the remarkably large British share of it (the pioneering) is often forgotten.' Such a contribution is reflected in the documentation of quilts held in the Museum collection. The Museum holds 39 Log Cabin quilts (Maison de bois rond), and of that number 31 are listed in the accession list as having an English, Scots or Irish 'Cultural Affiliation'. The oldest quilts in the collection include the circa 1860 Chevron shown on page 73; and a circa 1850 cotton coverlet given as a wedding gift to the bride of Donald MacKay of Yarmouth, Nova Scotia – a shipbuilder. Set in a diagonal furrow layout, the quilt is made of green, red, white and brown prints with a brown cotton binding. The Furrow layout was used on five quilts in the collection, Barn Raising on eight and Light and Dark on nine. One Light and Dark quilt – with a written inscription on the back ('For Harvey Hills made by Gramma in her 82nd year in the year 1883') is also given another name in the records - 'Sawlog'. The composition of lighter squares, however, appears like the Cross quilt shown on page 31. The Canadian collection also has three Fence Rail (sic) quilts, all dating from about 1900.

By whatever means, no one can deny that the Log Cabin pattern, in all its guises, has travelled a long and mysterious road. While factual answers to its adoption by quiltmakers may still be wanting, there is ample evidence of its journey from Britain and Scandinavia westward and 'Down Under' in the 19th century. Prior to that we have to rely on the evidence of other craft forms. The relationship of the Log Cabin quilt pattern to the much earlier craft of weaving awaits further research.

FOOTNOTES

2. Samuel Sharpe, *Egyptian Antiquities in the British Museum*, London 1862.
3. Henry Charles Shelly, *History of the British Museum*, London 1911.
4. John H. Taylor, *Death and the Afterlife in Ancient Egypt* London 2001, pg 90.
5. Carol Andrews, *Egyptian Mummies*, London 1998, pg 84.
6. Taylor, op cit, pg 60.
7. Eva Wilson, *Ancient Egyptian Designs*, London 2000, Illus 24, 25 and 26.
8. Ann Sutton, *The Structure of Weaving*, London 1982, pg 35.
9. Mary E. Black, *Key to Weaving*, New York 1949, p. 84.
10. Mary Meigs Atwater, *The Shuttle-craft Book of American Hand-weaving*, New York, 1966.
11. Ricky Clark, George W. Knepper and Ellice Ronsheim, *Quilts in Community, Ohio's Traditions.* Nashville 1991, pg 25.
12. H.W. Janson, *History of Art*, London 1995, pgs 111-112.
13. Owen Jones, *Grammar of Ornament*, London 1856. This edition London, 1986 pg 41 and Plate XXV.
14. Robert Field, *Geometric Patterns from Roman Mosaics*, Diss, Norfolk 1988, pg 16.

15. Thor Heyerdahl, *Early Man and the Ocean*, London 1978, pg 134.
16. Schnuppe von Gwinner, *The History of the Patchwork Quilt*, West Chester, Pa, 1988.
17. *Quilt Treasures The Quilters' Guild Heritage Search.* London 1995, pgs 154-155.
18. See An Moonen, *Quilts, the Dutch Tradition*, Arnhem, 1992.
19. Joan Foster, *Gamle Tekstiler. Lappeteknikk. Applikasjon. Quilting.* Halden, 2002.
20. Birgit Glüsing, personal correspondence dated 29 July 2002.
21. Asa Wettre, *Old Swedish Quilts*, Colorado, 1995, 32.
22. *Quilt Treasures*, opt cit, pages 115-116.
23. Ibid, pg 46.
24. Larch S. Garrad, 'Quilting and Patchwork in the Isle of Man' in *Folk Life,* Vol 17, 1979, pg 42.
25. Valerie Wilson, 'Quiltmaking in Counties Antrim and Down: Some Preliminary Findings from the Ulster Quilt Survey', *Uncoverings*, Vol 12 of the Research Papers of the American Quilt Study Group, 1991, pg 151.
26. See Ruth McKendry, *Quilts and Other Bed Coverings in the Canadian Tradition*, 1979, Plate 396.
27. See Margaret Rolfe, *Australian Quilt Heritage*, 1998, pgs 11-12.

28. Maurice de Sausmarez, *Basic Design: The Dynamics of Visual Form*, London, revised edition 2002, pg 17.
29. Mary Conroy, *300 Years of Canada's Quilts*, 1975, pg 28.
30. Jenny Manning, *Australia's Quilts, A Directory of Patchwork Treasures*, Hunters Hill, NSW 1999, pg 34.
31. Annette Gero, *Historic Australian Quilts*, Parramatta, 2000, page 56.
32. Janet Rae, *Quilts of the British Isles,* London 1987, pgs 110-111.
33. Gero, Op cit, pg 44.
34. Manning, op cit, pg 272.
35. Rolfe, op cit, pg 8.
36. Gero, op cit, pg 75.
37. Linda Welters and Margaret T. Ordonez, *Down by the Old Mill Stream*, tables, pg 5.
38. Ricky Clark, George W. Knepper and Ellice Ronsheim, *Quilts in Community*, Nashville 1991.
39. Fawn Valentine, *Echoes from the Hills*, Athens, Ohio, 2000.
40. Bets Ramsey and Merikay Waldvogel, *The Quilts of Tennessee*, 1986.
41. Sherrie F. Davidson, 'The Prince Edward Island Heirloom Quilt Survey: A Progress Report', *Patchwords*, 1994, pg 64.
42. Private correspondence dated 12 April 2003

THE CROSS
Australia

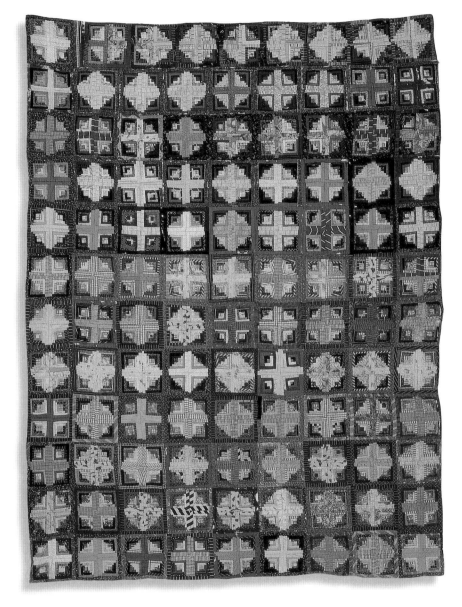

*Mixed fabric quilt by Hannah Rhodes,
Hindmarsh, South Australia, c.1900
166 x 231 cm (65 x 91in)
Courtesy of Joyce Walkley,
a descendant of the maker
(Photo by Michael Kluvanek)*

*Multi-coloured crosses,
Northern Ireland, c.1870
196 x 215cm (76 x 84in)
© National Museums and Galleries of
Northern Ireland, Ulster Folk &
Transport Museum*

The fine piecing by Hannah Rhodes illustrates a popular layout of the late 19th century – groups of four Log Cabin blocks sewn together in the shape of a cross. The use of an outlining strip or colour shading around the cross to provide emphasis was another feature, though not always practised. In the instance of the Turkey Red and white quilt (detail shown on page 118), such definition was not possible. The Cross layout was particularly popular in Britain, but whether there was any religious significance is unknown: perhaps it was simply easier to assemble, indiscriminately, groups of four blocks, then to worry about the placement of light and dark in a whole quilt top. Certainly the eight-inch crosses sewn by Hannah Rhodes give the traditional pattern quite a different look. The careful use of so many different cotton prints, wools, flannelette and furnishing fabrics has made each cross a jewel in its own right.

Another technique for making crosses was demonstrated by an unknown quiltmaker in Northern Ireland when she created a grid of coloured crosses. The red flannel centres of each block have been surrounded by strips of woven wool, silk and tartan. The backing is brown twilled cotton and the quilt is finished with bound edges and ties.

4 Blocks can also be made with larger corner squares and arranged diagonally first one way and then the other.

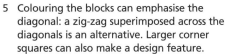

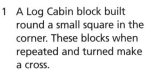

1 A Log Cabin block built round a small square in the corner. These blocks when repeated and turned make a cross.

2 The Cross can vary from a simple form where four logs are shaded in one colour to a more complex style such as a swastika. Alternating the colours of the cross (in this case orange and mauve) also relates to the Light and Dark layout on page 79.

3 The weave of the peg basket could easily have been the pattern source for this quilt. The blocks are arranged round a central cross with the diagonal of the blocks echoing the cross. The blocks in each corner of the quilt are set in one direction.

5 Colouring the blocks can emphasise the diagonal: a zig-zag superimposed across the diagonals is an alternative. Larger corner squares can also make a design feature.

6 Here the blocks are placed on the point and shaded to give a feeling of depth that might be seen in window panes.

7 This group shows blocks with a large centre and logs in a Courthouse Steps arrangement. The fabric sample shows four of these blocks making a cross. In the quilt design the cross is placed off-centre, top left, with the remaining blocks shaded to make borders around the cross. Alternatively, the cross could be placed centrally to give a very symmetrical design.

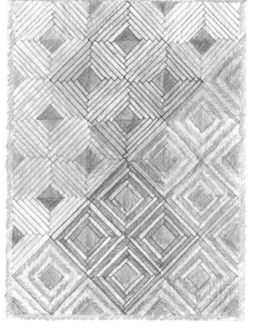

8 Here the design shows the blocks placed on the point, some shaded solidly with divided central squares and others with the logs in two shades giving a lighter feel to the cross.

Detail, ribbon 'Cross' c. 1870 185 x 205cm (71 x 80.5in) © National Museum and Galleries of Northern Ireland, Ulster Folk & Transport Museum

9 Detail from a Peruvian rug: the Inca Indians used the Log Cabin pattern as a base for their design, as a cross and as a dividing pattern in the form of faces.

10 Detail of a Log Cabin quilt by Janet Rae showing a cross with the central squares divided.

11 A cross created from striped ribbon showing an extra dimension to the use of fabric.

12 A pot of primulas was the starting
   point for Window over Provence

13 Drawings of the primulas
   developing into corner Log
   Cabin blocks within a circle.

 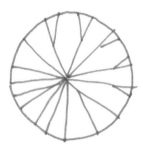 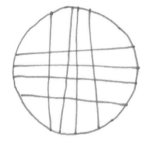 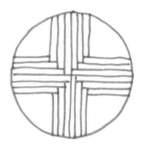

14 Exploring the Log Cabin corner
   blocks giving ideas for placing the
   block within or with various
   shapes.

15 Repeated blocks showing the basic
   plan for the quilt.

16 The initial idea is developed from a
   range of fabrics, with borders to
   give the feel of a window.

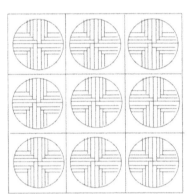

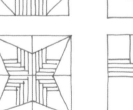 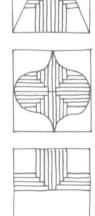

Window over Provence
Dinah Travis
114 x 114cm (45 x 45in)
(Photo by Michael Wicks)

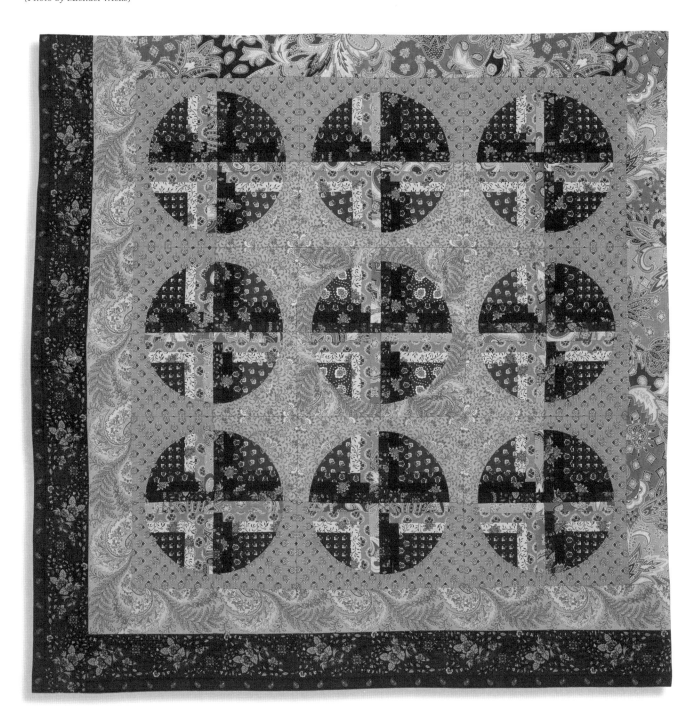

The inspiration for this quilt came from a pot of primulas and a collection of fabrics purchased on holiday in Provence. The fabrics are mainly in primary colours but not vibrant giving the feeling of warmth and sunshine. Some of the fabrics have border patterns and these have been used in wide borders. When the quilt came together the blocks looked like a window frame hence the name.

A contemporary vision of the cross theme is echoed here from yet another part of the world. The quiltmaker's 40th birthday began a process of reflection and decision making for the future. Having done her best in every endeavour, she decided the way forward was 'at her own pace'...doing something positive that gladdened both heart and mind.

Southern Cross
Reiko Hatakeyama, Miyagi, Japan
Hand and machine pieced, machine quilted cottons and polyester
177 x 205cm (69.5 x 83in)
Nihon Vogue Co Ltd
(Photo by Shunichi Nakamura)

HERRINGBONE
England

*Cotton and winceyette quilt,
England, c.1890
220 x 234 cm (86 x 91.5in)
© Copyright of The Quilters'
Guild of the British Isles*

One of the most recognisable weaves in suiting material is the herringbone, a twill which 'zig-zags'. The design concept is illustrated here in a quilt where the soft colours of winceyettes and printed cottons are haphazardly interspersed with a harder red. Another 'cousin' of the Log Cabin family, the pattern relies on lengths of slanted strips where colours meet in an unplanned fashion.

This use of a simple strip is perhaps more inventive than others. Often lengths were just sewn together to make a quilt top or table cover. The very serviceable 1930s Michigan quilt on page 103 was made for the owner from the family's dressmaking scraps and recycled clothing. In contrast are the Victorian ribbon quilts one finds in collections like the Ulster Folk & Transport Museum.

The herringbone design was used in suitings and often as a border on wool blankets made in Scotland, a practice taken to Canada by emigrant Scots weavers. Such blankets, with 'broken herringbone weave' borders are detailed in *Quilts*

*Close-up of herringbone border,
Scotland c.1860-1870,
205 x 246cm (80 x 96in)
Collection of Lindsay Hall*

and Other Bed Coverings in the Canadian Tradition by Ruth McKendry (1979). The example in the book, made of handspun and hand woven wool, dates from between 1825 and 1850 and is stated by McKendry to be 'characteristic of blankets found in Scottish areas... (of Canada).'

The adjacent close-up shows another bedcover with a herringbone border. This early quilt, which features the Log Cabin block set alternately with blocks divided into triangles, has two borders, the outside border being constructed of Log Cabin blocks turned on point.

1 The basic make-up of a Herringbone column. Start the column with a triangle at one end and build up by adding logs on each side.

2 A sample in old shirtings shows the construction of a single column

3 Columns can be coloured to appear like plaits or the left and right sides in different colours giving the impression of a third dimension.

4 The columns may vary in width and the angle of the logs made more or less acute.

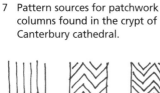

5 The columns may be coloured with alternate dark and light logs making zig-zags. Here the zigzags are blue with the alternate logs in a range of different colours.

6 The columns are ignored here. Colouring across the columns suggests a landscape of roofs.

7 Pattern sources for patchwork columns found in the crypt of Canterbury cathedral.

8 Herringbone logs are made uneven making the centre of the column swing from side to side.

9 The green-yellows, mauve-pinks and green-blues of the hydrangea plant were chosen for this design.

10 Logs are pink on one side and green-yellow on the other: placed alternately they make wavy columns.

11 Colouring across the design gives the effect of rock strata.

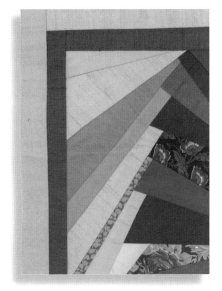

12 The wavy columns and the strata have been combined to make a more subtle quilt design.

13 Above: a fabric sample in silks, cotton and cotton prints showing the top left hand corner of design.

14 Abundant tree ferns in a Guernsey hotel garden inspired the quilt Fern.

15 Small rectangles show how columns can be placed in a quilt.

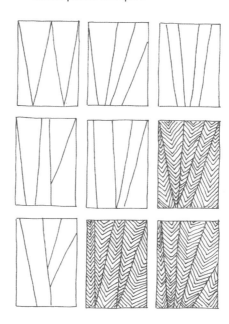

16 Below: computer drawings show the final possible shape.

17 a and b right: The shape of the quilt and the possible position of the logs together with a crayoned version.

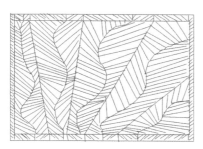

Fern
Dinah Travis
54 x 122cm (24 x 48in)
(Photo by Michael Wicks)

This quilt made from dupion silk, cottons dyed in a range of greens and commercial printed fabrics. The columns of the quilt were pieced quite freely altering the shapes of the logs as the sewing progressed to make the columns float and move like the fronds of the tree ferns. The colours chosen roughly follow the crayon drawing.

Perception is one of the major themes in the work of Barbara Macey and her adoption of the Log Cabin pattern as the basis of her work has provided endless opportunities for exploration. While some of her earlier pieces focused on op art, her 'Wave' series, of which Diversions is just one piece, has given her the opportunity to experiment with curves and the use of different widths of strips within one block.

Diversions
Barbara Macey, Australia
Wools, machine pieced
131 x 158cm (51.5 x 62 cm)
Collection of the National Wool Museum, Geelong

THE TILE
Northern Ireland

Silk, ribbon and brocade quilt, Northern Ireland, 1880 195 x 200.5cm(76 x 79in) © National Museums and Galleries of Northern Ireland, Ulster Folk & Transport Museum

The use of a dominant centre square is yet another design variable for the Log Cabin block. In this instance, the six-inch squares were begun with centres measuring 2.5 inches, although the blocks vary in size. Together with the method of assembly – piecing the blocks in long strips – there is an overall irregularity that perhaps reflects the maker's novice skills. And yet, this naiveté, together with the luxury fabrics, give it a certain charm. A label, carefully sewn with a herringbone stitch, and the names John and Mary, simply adds to its character. The backing, in contrast, is serviceable red linen and there is handquilting but no wadding.

The tile approach to the Log Cabin block – in this case with squares finished by a large triangle and turned on point – can also be seen in the Danish comforter by Maren Andersen of Northern Jutland. Well used and worn, this patchwork provides a fabric contrast to the Irish cover, for it is made of recycled clothing with patches sewn on a rough linen foundation. The quilt is filled with two types of tweed

Patchwork comforter by Maren Andersen, Denmark, c.1930 103 x 150cm (40 x 58.5 in) (Photo by Birgit Glüsing)

and backed with coarse reddish brown linen. The fabric composition of the quilt – bits and pieces from dresses, blouses, shirts and aprons – reflects the hard economic reality of the 1930s, when new materials were not readily affordable or even available. Although a simple construction, with only two logs surrounding the one square, the right choice of colour and fabric can give an overall distinctive appearance.

1 This quilt design is made from simple Log Cabin blocks. Two rounds of logs are built round a square with the same dimensions in the Courthouse Steps pattern. It lends itself to showing off the colours or the fabric of the logs.

2 The fabric sample shows a silk block enhanced with painted dots. There is a vast range of fabric dyes and paints on the market today.

3 The quilt design uses simple blocks with only one round of logs on point within a square.

4 A fabric sample showing one of the blocks with a marbled silk square. Cotton logs and triangles taking up the mauve colour from the marbling.

5 A computer drawing shows how the block in the next illustration multiplies into a quilt design.

6 Basic Log Cabin block taking on the simplicity of a tile block with limited colour and shading from dark to light.

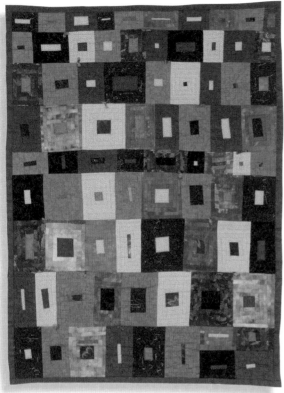

Jewel Kelim
Vine McGill, England
Pieced cottons with hand
quilting and orange silk ties.
66 x 91.5cm (26 x 36in)
(Photo by Michael Wicks)

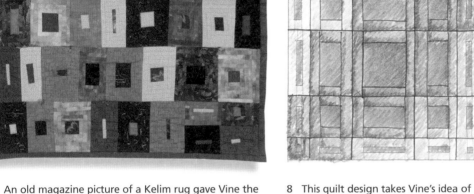 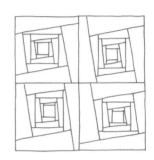

7   An old magazine picture of a Kelim rug gave Vine the inspiration she needed for this wallhanging. She combined her own hand dyed orange and blue-green strips with purchased fabrics to get the effect she wanted, finishing by quilting the irregular block centres and using orange silk to tie the layers more firmly together.

8   This quilt design takes Vine's idea of irregular blocks but organises them with the central block surrounded by gradually narrowing blocks. The technique makes the central block stand forward.

9   These blocks show that the logs need not have regular width strips. They take on a crazy and less static appearance.

10 Mavis has moved her blocks only slightly away from the square but enough to give a relaxed movement to the whole design.

Pennsylvanian Permutation
Mavis Haslem, England
Machine pieced and hand quilted
220 x 208cm (887 x 82in)

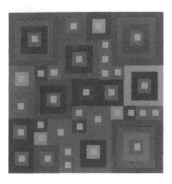 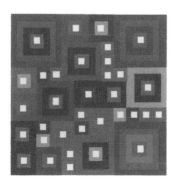

11 Two versions of the same quilt design show what happens when a simple colour change is made to the the central squares of the blocks: the blue ones recede into the general design while the yellow appear to float on top.

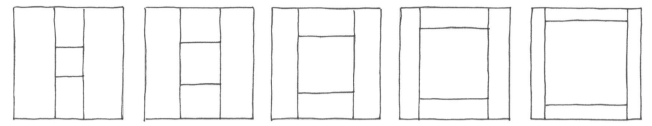

12 Simple Log Cabin blocks showing what
   happens when the proportions are changed.

13 A special selection of fabrics was chosen
   to make *Indigo Blues*.

15 The chosen blocks.

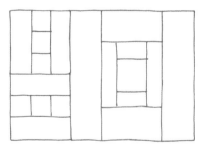

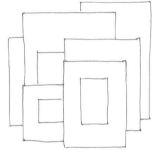

14 The photograph and the drawing show a
   stack of picture frames that could easily give
   the idea of varying sized rectangles. The
   rectangles could be used to design simple
   blocks that will display selected fabrics.

16 A drawing of the final quilt idea shows how
   red was added to give contrast to the blues.

This quilt shows off the beauty of the Japanese and African fabrics with a good balance between light and dark. The large circle in red makes a focal point supported by the small red square with big quilting stitches and red knotting.

Indigo Blues
Janet Rae
114 x 114cm (45 x 45in)
(Photo by Caleb Rutherford)

The golden days of late summer are represented with the use of doubled silk chiffon, silk organza, linen and dupion silk that has been embellished with rayon thread embroidery on both the fabric and dissolvable film. One of a series of hangings on the theme of transparency by this Dublin-based textile artist who uses traditional patterns for innovative quilts.

Indian Summer 2002
Ann Fleeton, Ireland
Machine pieced and embroidered, hand quilted
73 x 93cm (29 x 37in)

FURROWS
Isle of Man

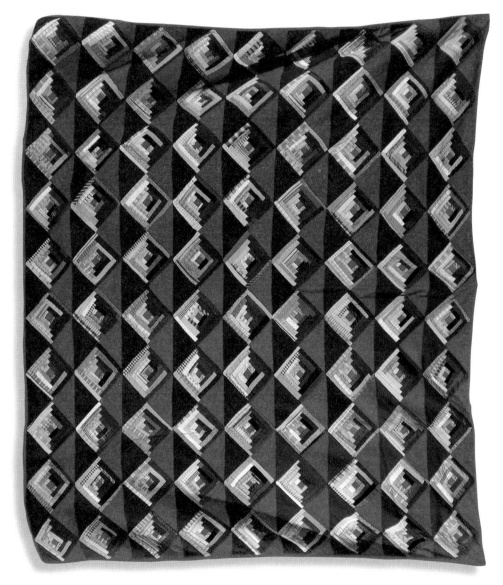

Woollen and cotton quilt by Isobel Gell, Peel, Isle of Man, 1912
163 x 230cm (64 x 80in)
Collection of Joan Thrussell
(Photo by The Manx Museum, Douglas)

Mixed fabric quilt by Olga Pedersen, Norway, c.1918.
130 x 165 cm (51 x 65in)
Reprinted by courtesy of N.W.Damm & Son (Photo by Helge Eek)

The creator of this unusual variation of a furrow layout worked in a shop where her aunt, a tailoress, also had a workroom. The quilt, pieced for Isobel's bottom drawer, includes a mix of shirt fabrics and is backed by two shades of indigo blue wool. Its layout is dominated by the indigo blue and red wool alternating squares, believed to be made from uniform material of the Manx Militia. Sadly, Isobel's fiancé died and the finished quilt was put away. Later, when she did marry, the quilt was passed down to her daughter Ella Quilliam and hence to the present owner.

Traditionally the furrow layout is either on the straight or the diagonal. As a variant, there are also parallel zig-zags (sometimes called Streak of Lighting) or, as seen overleaf, Snake Fence. Made in Ontario, of wool, silks and cotton, this quilt has no wadding and is backed with an Indian cotton bedcover. Its interest lies in the placing of the zig-zag lines.

The Straight Furrow quilt on the right shares an unusual feature with the Isle of Man quilt in that both have Log Cabin blocks set on point. Made in plain coloured wools, dress cottons, linen, silk and velvet, it is backstitched to a foundation but is neither quilted nor backed. It was sewn by Olga Pedersen. Widowed at a youthful age, Olga supported herself and her daughter by working in a newsagent's shop. But she was also an accomplished needlewoman and worked across several textile disciplines.

1 Basic blocks suitable for use in furrow quilts, square and on the point.

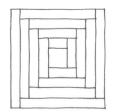

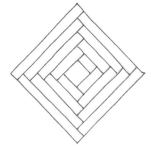

2 Layout of a straight furrow across the diagonal..

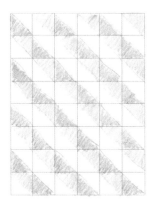

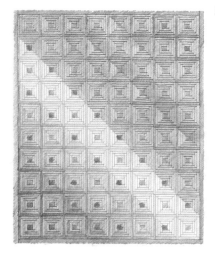

3 A straight furrow quilt design based on a rainbow. Individual furrows take colour from either side. The central squares of the blocks are red but another colour could be used or even shaded to show the changing colours of the rainbow.

Snake Fence, Canada, c.1900
168 x 178cm (66 x 70in)
© Canadian Museum of
Civilization, catalogue no. 79-6,
image no. S79-4119

4 Layout of a zig-zag furrow.

5 A zig-zag furrow quilt design coloured to give the hint of an asymmetrical layout.

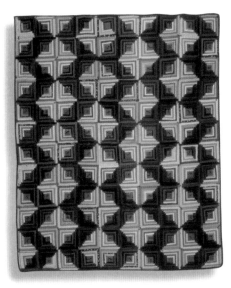

6 The zig-zag is the basis for many variations. In this Canadian example, the lines have been turned to form enclosures. The quilt is from the Frontenac District of Ontario and is listed in the Museum's accessions as being of English Canadian (canadienne anglaise) 'affiliation'.

7 Layout of a straight furrow with blocks on the point.

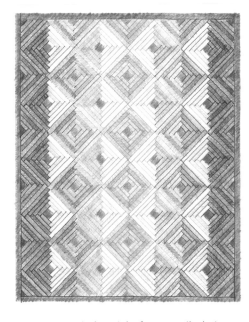

8 A symmetrical straight furrow quilt design with the blocks on the point coloured to give various weights of furrow.

9 Layout of a zig-zag furrow with blocks on the point.

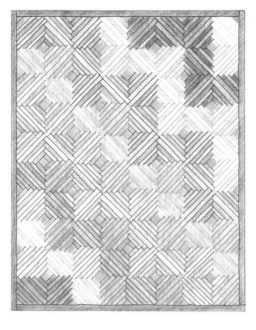

10 A diagonal zig-zag furrow quilt design with blocks on the point. The furrows are coloured red to pale orange from one corner and from purple to light mauve from the opposite corner.

All at Sea
Inger Milburn, England
Machine pieced, hand quilted
57 x 57cm (22.5 x 22.5in)

11 Inger calls this type of Log Cabin asymmetrical: with it she has created a feeling of the sea swell with three small sailing boats tossing on the surface.

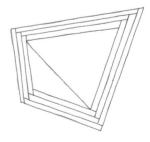

12 The roof of the Gare du Nord, Paris inspired Crevices. Nine asymmetrical blocks fit into one square and nine of these squares complete the quilt design. The squares give a stability to this design of jagged furrows.

13 Block from the centre of the nine asymmetrical blocks .

14 In-comimg tide on the French coast of the English Channel.

15 Lines of the waves, adjusted to suit the chosen curved patchwork block and finally superimposed on a grid.

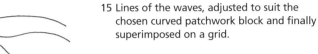

16 The curve of the block, logs drawn to fit the curve, and double logs replacing the wide logs to allow the use of a wider range of fabrics within each block. By using narrower logs it is possible to adopt a painter's approach to the choice of colour.

17 a & b
Two suggestions for colouring the design: in the first, each individual furrow changes from light blue to dark or dark blue to light and in the second each furrow has its own tonal value.

18 Fabric sample sewn to confirm the way of selecting fabric.

The Changing Tide
Dinah Travis
91cm x 91cm (36 x 36in)
(Photo by Michael Wicks)

This quilt is made from a wide range of printed fabrics
selected from a collection gathered over many years. Fabrics
were sorted into various tones of blue to blue-green for
specific furrows. The tiny yellow silk centre of each block
bounce forward or backward, depending on the tone of
neighbouring pieces, like flotsam on the waves.

Triple Aspect
Nikki Tinkler, England
Three-dimensional triptych, hand and machine
pieced and quilted, with dimpled pillows
147 x 100cm (58 x 39in)

Begun as a single bed quilt of miniature Log Cabin blocks,
this piece of work soon took on a life of its own. Using the
mathematical theory of chaos as her inspiration, Nikki
Tinkler portrayed formality with vertical rows of colour and
tones in the left panel. The central panel shows the small
blocks breaking free before finally reaching a softened
formality. First prize winner in geometrics, National Quilt
Championships, 2001.

PINEAPPLE
Scotland

*Cotton quilt by Helen Dinwoodie Maclachlan, Scotland, c.1895
100 x 120cm (78 x 86in)
Private Collection*

*Close-up of red flannel, cotton and wool quilt, Northern Ireland, c. 1875
183 x 211cm (72 x 83in)
National Museums and Galleries of Northern Ireland, Ulster Folk & Transport Museum*

As crisp and fresh as the time it was made, this red, white and blue Pineapple quilt, with frill, was a family project. It was sewn over many winter evenings by the fire (and the light of an oil lamp) by Helen Maclachlan and her daughters Marion, Mary and Margaret. The family lived in Thornhill, Dumfriesshire, Scotland's southwest corner, where Mary's husband John worked as a builder and roofer. Descendants of the family do not know where Helen learned her sewing skills or indeed if they had been passed down by her mother. Helen's father was chief forester to the Duke of Buccleuch, a family title which continues to the present day and represents Scotland's largest landowner.

The Pineapple Log Cabin does not appear with any frequency among British Log Cabin quilts but examples can be found in public collections. The early quilt from Larne, believed to date from about 1840, is in the collection of the Ulster Folk & Transport Museum. Unlike the Scottish quilt,

where the spiky edges reminiscent of the tropical fruit appear in white, the Irish example has black spikes. The red flannel centres of each block are surrounded by a mixture of cotton and wool. A rather more sombre name has been used in Northern Ireland for a red and white version of the Pineapple – Soldier's Wreath. Given the pattern's likeness to the traditional poppy wreaths laid on British war memorials, it is an understandable reference.

1 Basic Pineapple block and fabric sample showing the shapes from which the name is derived.

2 Four blocks showing how they combine to make a continuous layout.

3 An arrangement of pine cones reflecting the layout.

4 Circles can be suggested by different colouring of the logs.

5 Another colouring shows interlocking swirling shapes.

6 From Inger's prize winning quilt at Quilt Expo 2 exploiting the curved shape using straight logs.

Detail, Turkish Garden 2
Inger Milburn, England
102 x 140cm (40 x 55in)

7 & 8
Two designs show how the Pineapple layout can be coloured to emphasise a central rosette.

9 Pat has created a garden which one could imagine walking through, stopping to enjoy the different colours.

Pineapple Path
Pat Taylor, England
70 x 70cm (28 x 28in)

10 The colouring here makes the Pineapples spin round. Compare their shape with the natural pineapple.

11 Photograph of a sunset over the
French countryside.

12 Torn paper strips recording
the colours of the sunset.

13 Rich colours selected from
a ragbag of fabrics.

14 The quilt design reflecting the movement of
the colours in the sunset: grey-purples of the
static landscape with pinks through orange
to yellow of the sky.

15 A layout of varying shaped blocks
considered for Sunset but rejected.

Sunset
Janet Rae
30ins x 30ins (76cm x 76cm)
(Photo by Michael Wicks)

A vast number of colours have been used as in a painting, to create the movement of the changing sky at sunset. This number of colours can only be found in a collection of fabrics made over many years.

The title of this quilt is a tribute to all the sewers who have started patchwork by making a hexagon quilt and been put off for life! Using a mixture of silk and cotton, to vary the reflection of light, Irene turned the tropical 'fruit' into large silk flowers that run across the quilt's surface.

Not a Grandmother's Flower Garden
Irene MacWilliam, Northern Ireland
Silk and cotton, machine pieced, hand quilted
132 x 193cm (52 x 76in)

ILLUSION
Wales

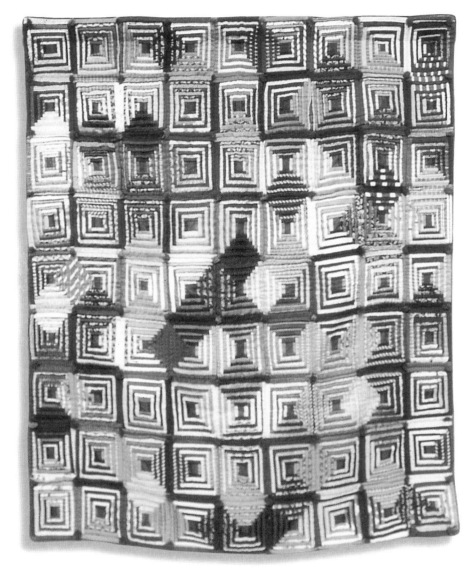

Mixed fabric quilt from the Morgan family, Wales, 1888
168 x 198cm (66 x 78in)
Jen Jones Collection

Trouser, tie and other wools in stripes
and tartan, Scotland, c.1900
197 x 199cm (77 x 78in)
Perth Museum & Art Gallery

The challenge of using colour and fabric to 'play games' with visual perception is just one of many avenues that have been pursued in the Log Cabin layout. The Welsh quilt above demonstrates this quality, although the unknown maker probably achieved the eclectic mix by chance rather than intent.

At one glance, this quilt might appear as a collection of Japanese lanterns. At another, the perception changes and there would appear to be an attempt to pursue a light and dark theme. Some of the darker blocks in fact, seem to float across the surface. Then there is the use of white linen as alternate strips in some blocks – these act as highlights or outlining devices and add yet another challenge to our visual experience. A generation ago, this quilt allegedly rested, not on a bed, but the back of a Victorian sofa. What an addition to the family parlour!

The Scottish quilt, with its Turkey Red or blue wool centred blocks, gives yet another sensation. Although it has been put together in a Light and Dark layout, the fabric in the six-inch blocks has been cut to ensure the stripes are angled, not straight. Thus one experiences a feeling of discord caused by the jagged look – due entirely to the white or pale colours of individual strips that seem to leap in all different directions. The overall impression would have been much more placid if the striped fabrics had been cut at right angles or on the straight.

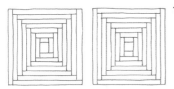

1 Basic blocks for use in any of these ideas.

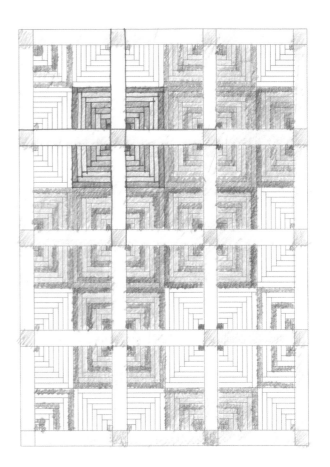

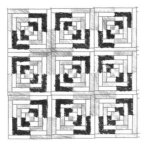

2 Ideas here make some of the logs appear superimposed on others.

3 Sashing in this design floats above the off-centre blocks which appear to link with others to make larger ones.

City by the Sea
Inger Milburn,
England
122 x 158cm
(48 x 62in)

4 Here the logs are added to one side of the block first followed by the second and so on. When the blocks are turned and joined together it gives the illusion of weaving.

5 Inger uses off-centre and irregular Log Cabin blocks to create a seascape with houses huddled together on the shore. Commercial and hand-dyed cottons are machine pieced and quilted.

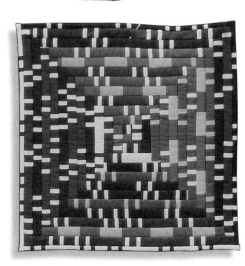

6 Sample of striped fabric used in one large Log Cabin block creating a static almost architectural feel, possibly a crowded town landscape of modern tower blocks.

Hyena Stomp, 1962
Frank Stella
© ARS, NY and DACS, London 2003

7   This painting captures the elements of design that is needed for quilts. The lines of the painting would make the pattern for a block, and the arrangement of the colour suggests a square spiral figure.

8   Four triangles make up the block: two triangles are similar but the other two are different. The result is a square spiral.

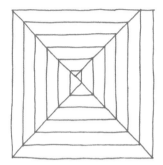

9   Two ideas: one using the square spiral and the other an attic window colourway.

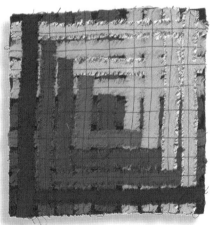

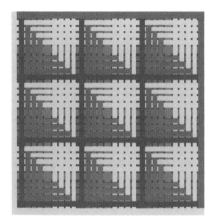

10 A weaving: logs woven into a block with each log sewn through the middle, making a grid that secures it all.

11 The logs are laid in the formation of a traditional Log Cabin block with a small space between each one, finally sewing through each log to secure to a foundation square. The logs are woven in a similar way to the bindings of the Egyptian mummies.

12 This design shows how the weaving can be continued across several blocks.

13 Many photographs of flowers, together with a love of the colour indigo and the Welsh quilt were the inspiration behind The Secret Garden.

14 A collection of large fabric prints, reflecting colours seen in the flowers, with some old denim.

15 Various colourings were made of the background squares.

16 This shows where the denim was to be used, and the chosen block.

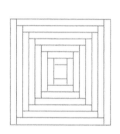 

17 The denim idea was superimposed over the free arrangement of coloured squares. To complete the design indigo tassels were used to knot the whole together.

Cut-up large prints lend themselves to showing movement and a variety of shapes. Here they represent the foliage as partially seen through a lattice fence. Hence the name. The tassels are holding the fence together, as string is often used in a garden.

The Secret Garden
Dinah Travis
40ins x 52ins (102cm x 132cm)
(Photo by Michael Wicks)

Based on a series of photographs, this garden shows how colours change as the seasons progress. The bird and Indian lady are pieces of garden sculpture and the quilting patterns include leaves, spiders, butterflies and a cat. The Log Cabin squares were constructed on paper which was then removed and the quilt was machine quilted from the back with invisible thread in the bobbin.

A Year in the Garden
Angela Chisholm, Scotland
Silk and cotton fabrics
127 x 137cm (50 x 54in)

TRIANGLES
Canada

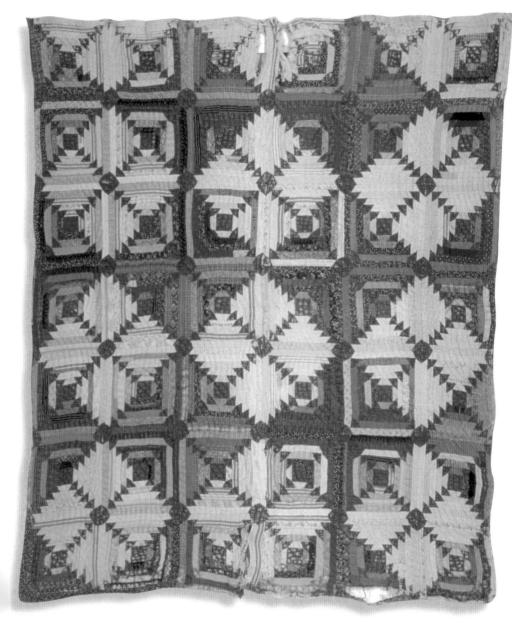

Wild Goose Chase, Hartington,
Ontario, c.1875
145 x 167cm (57 x 66 in)
© Canadian Museum of
Civilization, catalogue no. 79-21,
image no. S79-4134

Pieced quilt with triangles,
Co Antrim, c.1890
© National Museums and
Galleries of Northern Ireland,
Ulster Folk & Transport Museum

Log Cabin blocks with applied shapes are a rarity and this early example, believed to have been made sometime between 1851 and 1875, poses more questions than it answers. Red triangles have been applied from corner to corner, giving the effect of the pieced pattern called Flying Geese – a pattern often used for quilt borders. Had the unknown maker been partly influenced by seeing a pieced Pineapple Log Cabin block? Certainly the use of appliqué dictated that it would be labour intensive. Made of cotton, with a black cotton print backing and cotton wadding, the quilt has another unusual feature: it is quilted in a fan design. Many early Log Cabin quilts had neither wadding nor quilting. They were often just tied at regular intervals. Another Log Cabin quilt in the Canadian Museum of Civilization collection, made about 1860 in a Light and Dark layout, also features quilting – in a shell pattern.

Although the pieced version of the Irish Flying Geese patch starts in the manner of a Pineapple block – a square with triangles on either side – the similarity ends with the corners. Successive layering of strips across corners give the Pineapple block rounded instead of acute angles, thus a sense of whirling movement which is seen in many of the Pineapple quilt examples. The Irish patchworker who pieced the Turkey Red and white quilt in County Antrim worked with a less ambitious palette of colour than her Canadian counterpart, but the dynamics of the finished quilt were equally as impressive.

1 Log Cabin block with Geese.

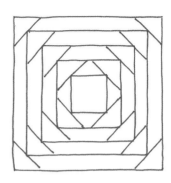

2 Two colourways of white Flying Geese over a traditional dark and light Log Cabin and a traditional Courthouse Steps pattern.

4 The orange Geese fly through a white passage against a mauve sky.

Crossing the Borders
Irene MacWilliam, Northern Ireland
Machine pieced using cottons and
polycottons
206 x 206cm (81 x 81in)

3 The coloured triangles, which run across the blocks, denote the Flying Geese which cross the boundaries of many countries, unaffected by politics, skin colour or language.

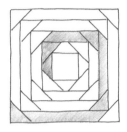

5 Selecting pieces within the block suggests curves: dart board and hook designs.

6 Black and white Geese fly over a coloured dart board pattern.

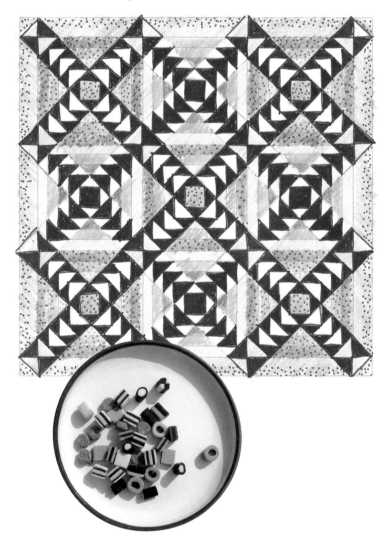

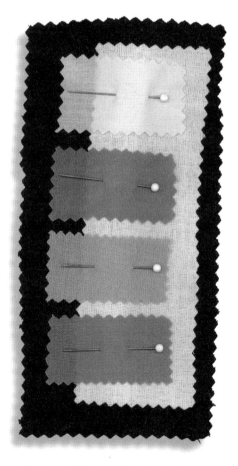

7 Cotton fabric swatches in the clear liquorice allsort colours.

8 The rich colours of this drawing suggest the colour for Flight from India.

9 Variations showing different ways to set out the triangles.

10 Sample of sumptuous dark magenta and yellow silk dupions used for *Flight from India*.

11 *Flight from India* design showing the geese crossing at right angles.

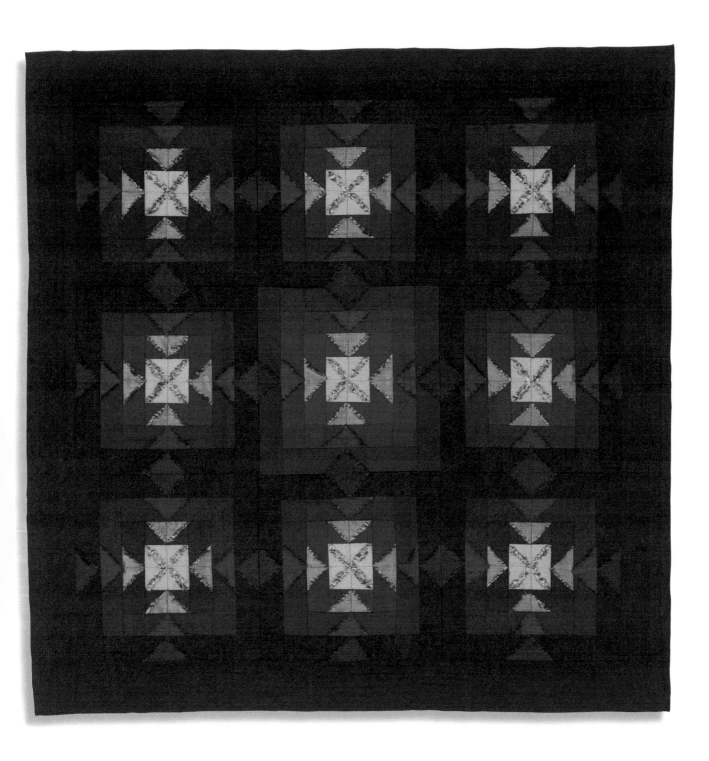

Silk dupions suggest the vibrant colours of the India continent. The geese triangles are sewn into the seams of the Log Cabin block, and stitched across to secure them with the bias edges left free to fray. The quilt symbolises not birds but the daily flights of peoples between India and Britain.

Flight from India
Dinah Travis
28ins x 28ins (71cm x 71cm)
(Photo by Michael Wicks)

Crossroads Number 2
Judy Hooworth, Australia
Machine pieced and hand and machine quilted.
244cm (96 in) square.

Instead of triangles, Judy Hooworth has used purple squares at the end of each log to create the diagonal cross. 'I love Log Cabin designs and red and yellow quilts and wanted to combine the two in a complex arrangement using many different red, yellow and purple prints and values,' explained Judy. Her elaborate piecing was further enhanced by splitting each section of four blocks with more sashing and joining squares. The outside borders and the sashing between each group of four blocks are African prints.

CHEVRON
Canada

*Pieced wool, silk and cotton,
Kingston, Ontario, c.1860
140 x 192 cm (55 x 76in)
© Canadian Museum of
Civilization, catalogue no. 79-21,
image no. S79-4134*

*Amish doll's bed quilt in cotton,
Indiana, c.1870
Classic Antiques, Osceola, Indiana*

Although the strips are not as regular as those executed in wood inlay by the 18th century French cabinetmaker on page 11, Mrs Spencer, the maker of this Chevron quilt, was following the same practice of placing strips across a square. The result has a slightly irregular and almost contemporary appearance. The charm (and the fun) of this Log Cabin 'cousin' lies in the unpredictable joining of individual squares. Strips may be regular in width but squares don't always match up and the centre is often cockeyed. It is, however, a 'fast and economical sew', which is why many class this quilt as utilitarian.

The Amish doll's bed quilt on the right was made a decade or so after the quilt by Mrs Spencer and is much more regular in appearance with large triangles at either end of a square. String quilts, a particular favourite in North America, are often much freer. A survey recorded in *The Quilts of Tennessee* by Bets Ramsey and Merikay Waldvogel (Nashville, 1986) indicated that string quilts accounted for almost five per cent of the pieced quilts category. They are particularly associated with the American Depression and were also often a 'first time' quilt for children learning how to sew. The technique is simple: remnants or 'strings' of irregular widths, some wedge shaped, are sewn on a paper or cloth foundation by the stitch and flip method. Such free assembly and use of brightly coloured prints sometimes made the string square more difficult to decipher when assembled (see page 75).

1   Basic Rail Fence blocks

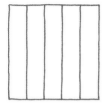 

2   Sample of four Rail
    Fence blocks.

3   The quilt design shows how the Rail Fence
    block can appear to weave like the cane on
    baskets, make plaited strings cross the quilt
    diagonally, and resemble a border depending
    how they are coloured.

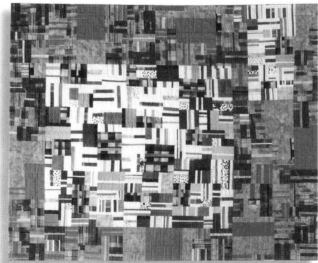

*Impressions of Summer
Chiyo Nakagawa, Toyama,
Japan162 x 205cm (63.5 x 78in)*

4   To escape the long dull winter in the
    Hokuriku area of Japan, Chiyo turned her
    thoughts to summer and used her
    imagination to capture the essence of bright
    hot days.

5   Various ways of using
    the logs: combining the
    diagonal with the
    straight, using different
    angles and introducing
    the plain half triangle.

6 Basic diagonal block and showing how, when combined with turned blocks, it makes a Chevron.

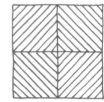

8 A Roman Stripes block which introduces the plain half triangle.

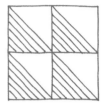

7 Various colourings of the Chevron arrangement can make dart board blocks, windmills, counter-changed squares, quarter and half triangles, and borders.

9 Sample of Roman Stripes also known as Streak of Lightning particularly when the diagonal is emphasised.

American String Quilt c.1940
My Quilt Space, Canton, Illinois

10 Assorted cottons in irregular strings put together in Chevron-style blocks which are often hard to analyse in terms of pattern.

Chevron Quilt made in 1983 by the patchwork class of the Bromley Adult Education College for St Christopher's Hospice, South East London. Made from scraps except for a single green strip across the centre of each block to help unify the broad range of colours.

12 Inspiration for *Forest*: a drawing of leafless trees from a local wood and a photograph of a modern stairwell showing similar uprights and diagonals.

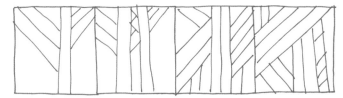

13 Tree drawing adapted for patchwork

14 Blocks designed from the tree drawings.

15 Four chosen blocks.

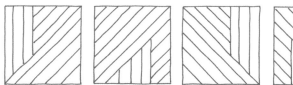

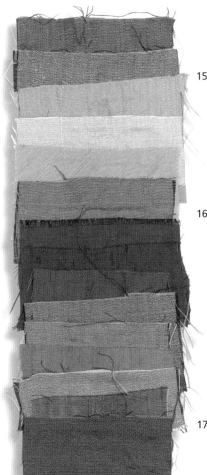

16 Chosen range of silk dupion.

17 Design for Forest with the four blocks turned and placed to give the impression of a deep wood reinforced by the colours arranged from dark at the base to light at the top.

Forest
Dinah Travis
31ins x 31ins (79cm x 79cm)
(Photo by Michael Wicks)

The leafless trees have formed the basis for this quilt but the basic structure of pattern-making, integral to traditional quiltmaking, is still evident. Hints of the Chevron appear among the trees.

The floor of the Barbican Theatre in London provided the initial inspiration for this quilt, which gained in theatricality as it progressed: the movement of colour across the surface denotes the play of footlights, while the black Harlequin diamonds and inset folded triangles in blue complete a feeling of drama.

Barbican by Pat Salt, England
Cotton, machine pieced
163 x 230cm (64 x 90.5in)
(Photo by Michael Wicks)

LIGHT AND DARK
United States

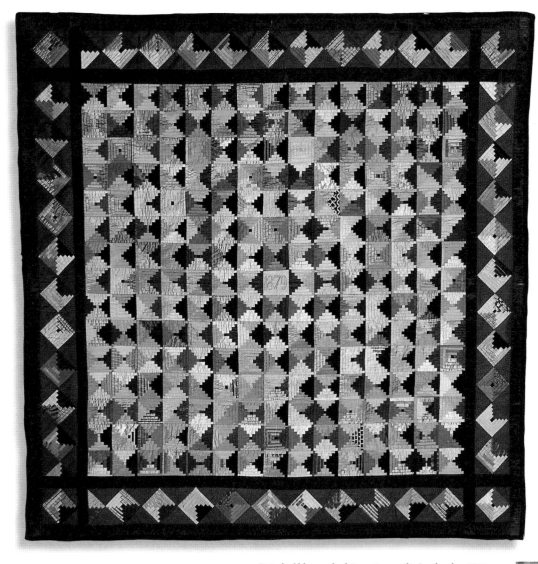

Silk quilt by a member of the McCutchen family, Kentucky. Embroidered date 1879 178cm (70in) square. Collection, Kentucky Library and Museum, Western Kentucky University, Bowling Green, Ky. (Photo by Jim Roshan)

Detail of blue and white cotton quilt, Scotland, c.1870 175 x 211cm (69 x 83in). Author's Collection

Shading and a division into light and dark is the very essence of the Log Cabin quilt. It is the repeat use of these values that gives us so many different options when it comes to assembling a layout. The Courthouse Steps variation is also apt to follow a Light and Dark theme, although in the case of the McCutchen quilt, placement of blocks is more chance than planned. This is a very fine example of the Victorian seamstresses' art. The individual squares are small – only 3.5 inches – and the silk logs or strips are narrow. The blocks in the border, which almost resemble small envelopes, have been turned on point and framed by black borders. One can imagine the exquisite care taken with this luxury covering – not only with the making but also with its subsequent use.

By contrast, the cotton quilt from Ayrshire in Scotland has been well used and washed. It too follows the Light and Dark theme. What makes this quilt interesting is its method of construction. Strips are not sewn side to side but folded, overlapped and stitched to a foundation. Nor does each block have a centre square. Sometimes quiltmakers used the backing as their starting point or square – simply laying strips down in a square formation. Many say that quilts made by the folded technique are stronger and last longer. Certainly the doubling of strips makes for extra durability, especially with fabrics like silk, satin and velvet.

1 Traditional Light and Dark quilt design with the colours shading diagonally from yellow to orange and dark to light mauve. The final logs of the blocks together with squares act as sashing for the quilt. This quilt could be easily assembled with blocks like the one shown here of frayed silk logs or blocks in the traditional method.

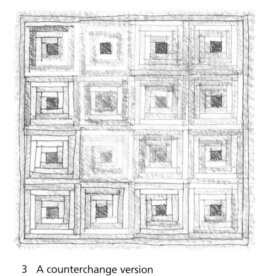

2 Various layouts on the Light and Dark theme.

3 A counterchange version of Light and Dark.

4 A block in which the logs on two sides have been changed, and a design using this block to making a floral centre with fan shapes around.

5 A block where all the logs are at an angle with a design showing how it makes flower shapes.

7 A traditional four blocks showing a darker centre.

8 A central Log Cabin with logs in each round all one colour making a medallion surrounded by four triangle Log Cabins with logs of the same light colour only on two sides.

6 The petals of a rose show how shapes can pivot round a centre.

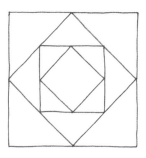

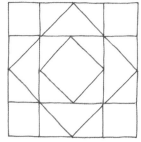

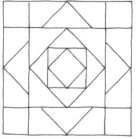

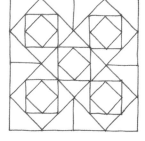

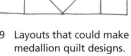

9 Layouts that could make medallion quilt designs.

10 Quilt design showing how the logs are placed in each shape to emphasise the medallion layout.

Arioso
Dinah Travis
180 x 180cm
(72 x 72in)

'Oh Grateful Colours
Bright Looks'
Sheila Yale, England
152 x 228cm
(60 x 90in)

11 One in a series of quilts made in a Log Cabin medallion layout. One shape appears to float on top of the next with a final border made from strips echoing those in the main section.

12 Sheila uses a wide range of unusual and interesting fabrics that many other quilters would discard. Here she gives the feeling of one layer upon another.

13 Photograph of quilts over a
rail, the source for Two in One.

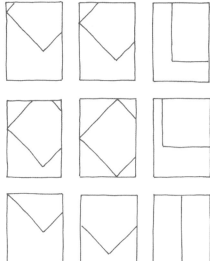

14 Possible layouts for the quilt.

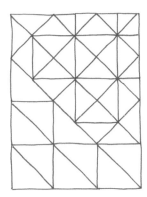

15 Plan of blocks in the
chosen layout.

16 Chosen range of silk
dupion for the top quilt.

17 Welsh wools for
the basic quilt.

18 Design showing one quilt
sitting on the other.

The ideas behind this quilt were to show the old fabrics against the new, to oppose traditional technique with new thinking, and to show everyday against best.

Two in One
Dinah Travis
66 x 86cm (26 x 34in)
(Photo by Michael Wicks)

Bridget used a wool foundation on which to sew her wool samples and finished the back by covering the seams with strips of wool. 'The size of each centre was dictated by the size of the sample in the first block,' she commented. 'It happened in a very leisurely manner. I was experimenting and using the quilt-as-you-go method.' A pair of Bridget's trousers also found a new life in the quilt... which with its weight aptly performs its basic function of keeping sleepers warm.

But Baby It's Cold Outside
Bridget Ingram-Bartholomaus, Germany
Wools, machine pieced
156 x 200cm (61.5 x 79in)

STEPS
Norway

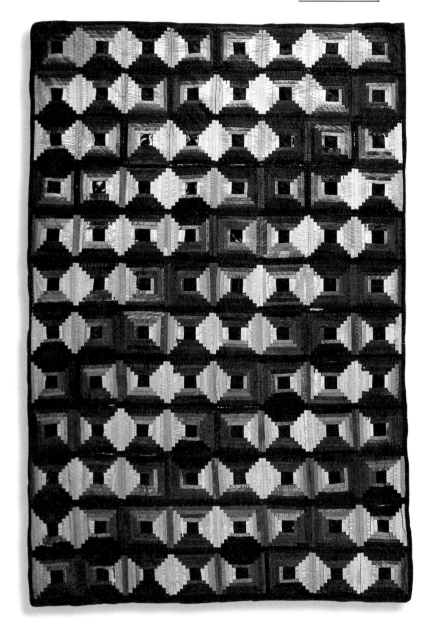

*Silk and velvet steps quilt cover by
Mathilde Schjander, Oslo, c.1870
130 x 190 cm (51 x 74.5in)
Reprinted by courtesy of N.W. Damm
& Son (Photo by Helge Eek)*

*Bow tie Log Cabin, English, c.1890
80 x 100 cm (31.5 x 39 in)
Collection of Ron Simpson*

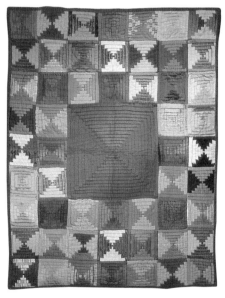

Sewn as a blanket case with button fastenings, this patchwork was one of two twin bed coverlets made as wedding presents for Fredrikke and Ole Larsen, and recorded during the Norwegian quilt documentation. Over the years the patchwork cases were used, however, for both warmth and as wallhangings, before they were finally handed down to the maker's great-great-granddaughter, who gave them to the present owner.

The Steps variation of Log Cabin is easily worked by placing strips on opposite sides of a square, rather than sewing strips in succession around each side. It is probably the easiest of the Log Cabin techniques to execute and yet, in terms of late 19th century popularity, the least used. The technique provides quite different pattern opportunities for layout. The Norwegian patchwork has a particular lustre because of the use of silk. The predominant pale colours form a kind of globe or ball. The black centres of each block slip into the background so that the balls, albeit a mix of light and dark, are uniform across the surface. Turned the other direction, and with red replacing the black centres, the balls become the Japanese or Chinese lanterns shown in the following design notes.

The bow tie crib quilt of twilled cottons and wool is backed with a geometric floral printed cotton. Both quilts demonstrate the effectiveness of using plain coloured fabrics as opposed to the usual Log Cabin tradition of concentrating on tonal qualities while mixing many different prints.

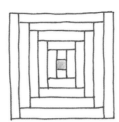 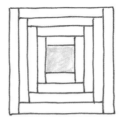 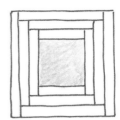 

1 Four basic blocks showing different sized central squares.

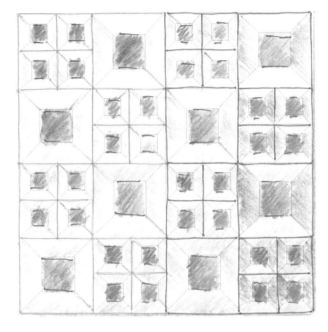 

2 Two layouts: the larger central square in the first drawing gives a feeling of columns or piles of cotton reels. In the second drawing, the smaller square makes the diagonal a dominant feature.

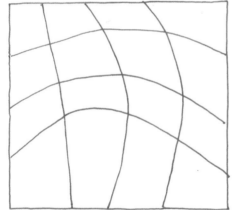

3 A grid of wavy lines into which to build Log Cabin blocks.

4 Blocks set on the wavy grid give the appearance of the central shapes receding, like steps down into a pool. Careful planning, well drawn blocks and ordered sewing techniques would be needed to execute this idea. The colour possibilities are endless.

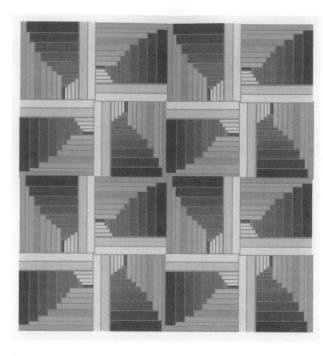

6 Design showing groups of step blocks making windmills.

5 Blocks of steps into the beyond.

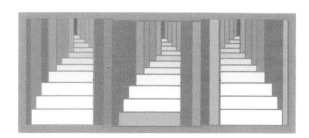

7 Three blocks showing how colour helps the steps to disappear up into the distance, and how the grading of the size of steps gives the impression of a curve and perspective.

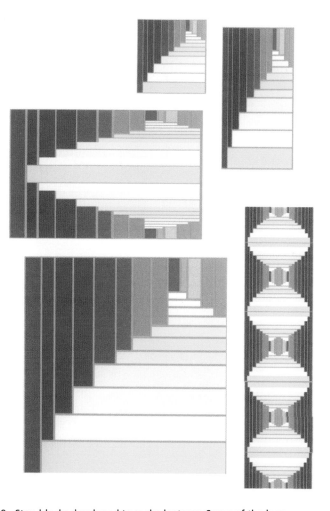

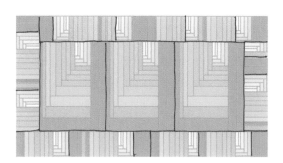

8 Set of three blocks in sugar almond colours with an echoing border.

9 Step blocks developed to make lanterns. Some of the logs in the original block have been illuminated and four blocks are turned and joined for the curves to become the round shape of a lantern.

Detail, woollen
lanterns, Scotland,
c. 1930
168 x 182cm
(66 x 71.5cm)
Collection of
Lindsay Hall

10 A quilt design of hanging lanterns led to the idea of a wall quilt consisting of individual hangings.

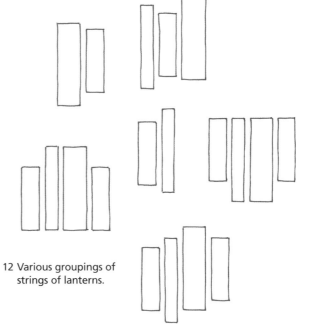

12 Various groupings of strings of lanterns.

13 Lantern block and sample showing how the width of the logs changes.

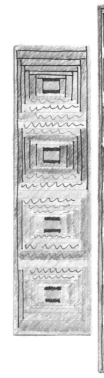
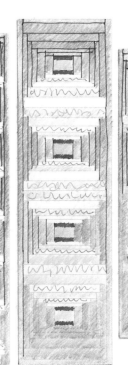
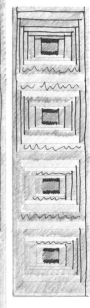

14 Final design for *Hanging Lanterns*.

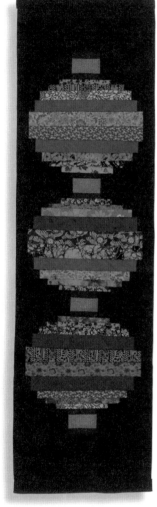

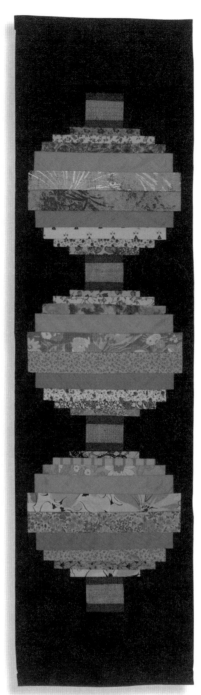

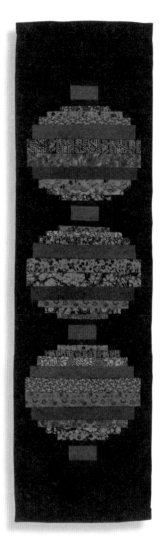

Hanging Lanterns.
Dinah Travis
31 x 34in (79 x 86cm)
(Photo by Michael Wicks)

The idea for this quilt came from hanging a quilt in a stairwell and being able to hang the individual section at various heights. A mixture of over-dyed prints for rich turquoises, Liberty lawns for fine piecing, dupion silk to add a sense of luxury and dark cottons for contrasting background were the chosen fabrics.

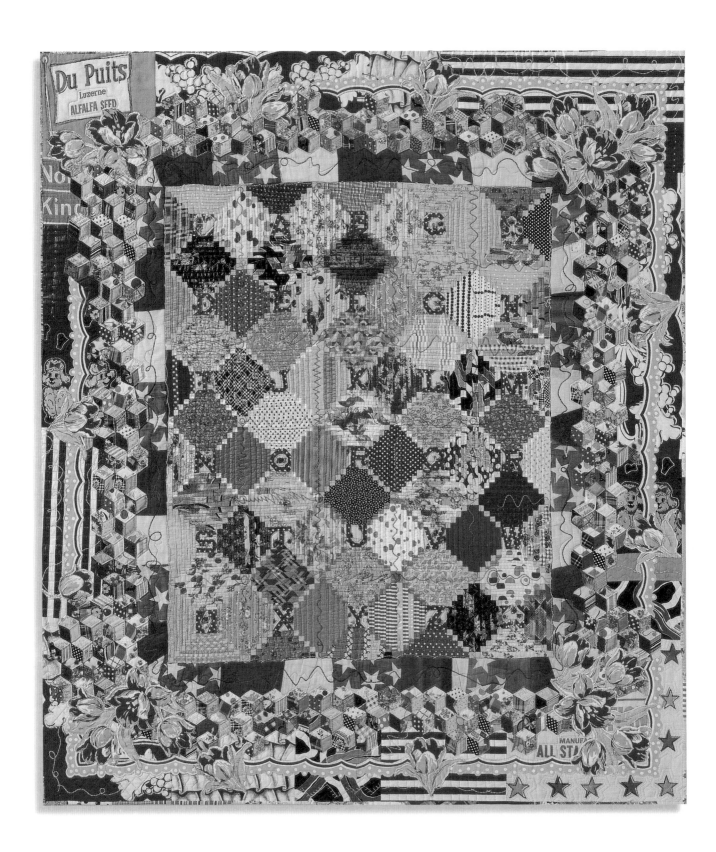

Memories of growing up and time spent in her own room inspired Keiko to express her nostalgia through the Steps pattern. Using old fabrics - silks, cottons and polyesters – she recorded her feelings about the favourite records she played, an unsuccessful love story, favourite stars and the difficult maths she had to study – everything associated with her room.

In My Room
Keiko Torii, Aichi, Japan
Hand pieced, appliquéd, quilted and embroidered
173 x 195cm (68 x 76in)
Nihon Vogue Co Ltd
(Photo by Shunichi Nakamura)

THE OFF-CENTRE BLOCK
Sweden

*Quilt by Tilda Halling,
Medelpad, Sweden, c.1920
137 x 197 cm (55 x 79 in)
Collection of Asa Wettre*

*Close-up of quilt made in Australia by
Nicholes Wallace, c.1895
234cm x 236cm (92 x 93 in)
National Pioneer Women's Hall of
Fame, Alice Springs*

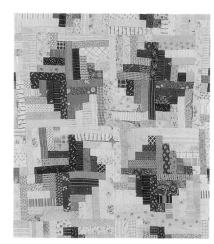

Historically, the Off-Centre Log Cabin block seems an invention of the late 19th and early 20th centuries. Extant examples of old quilts that deviate from the usual centre square surrounded by strips are rare.

Any shape can be used to begin an off-centre square, as seen in the example made by Tilda Halling, a farmer's wife. Although it appears to include some Pineapple techniques, the block is actually begun with a pointed rectangle in the corner with four blocks together forming a cross.

Asa Wettre, the current owner of the quilt, describes the industrious life of the Halling family in her book *Old Swedish Quilts*. Although well-to-do, Tilda worked alongside and supervised the maids who had an active role in all the family's textile activities – knitting, weaving and sewing. It was a busy household where quiltmaking was a continuous process. The origin of this particular off-centre block is unknown, but one of its curiosities, as discussed on page 18, is its translation to America as the 'Grandmother's Quilt' pattern.

A more conventional square was used to begin each block in the coverlet made by another farmer's wife, Nicholes Wallace of Carlston, Victoria. The Light and Dark layout of the quilt is enhanced by the use of bright blues and reds and, unusually, the foundation technique of sewing was not used, nor was the coverlet backed. Believed to have been sewn for a son and daughter-in-law, the coverlet boasts another unusual feature – a wide pieced border (see full quilt on p.118).

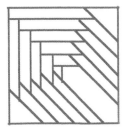

1   Basic Swedish block and sample showing the cross made by four turned and joined blocks

2   Making the logs in the corner opposite the starting shape very dark or contrasting in colour creates circles that dominate the pattern

3   Colouring alternate sections of the block with contrasting colours gives a three dimensional feel with the cross floating on top. Making the blocks appearing less static and possibly start to spin.

4   This drawing shows that a completely different shape is obtained by making the cross and the logs in the opposite corners one tone or colour. All the blocks begin to link up forming a grid which is like a parquet floor.

5   A halo effect is made by colouring around the cross. The colours can go from light to dark to make the cross stand up or from dark to light for the reverse effect.

6 An emphasis on the vertical possibilities of the combined blocks making columns. This is only a beginning; columns could be made fatter or narrower, horizontal contrasted with vertical.

7 An Art Deco style reminiscent of the early cinema architecture. Note the different shapes made by the shading of the opposite sides of the block.

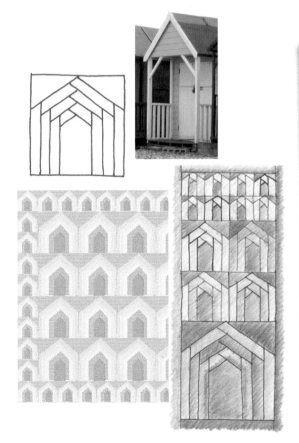

8 The off-centre shape has been placed centrally at the base suggesting brightly coloured beach huts.

9 Although made using the Attic Window technique, this quilt could just as easily have been constructed as an Off-centre Log Cabin. The choice of Nancy Crow fabric and shading make the impact.

City of Lights
Rita Bos-Croes, Belgium
124 x 134cm (48.5 x 52.5in)

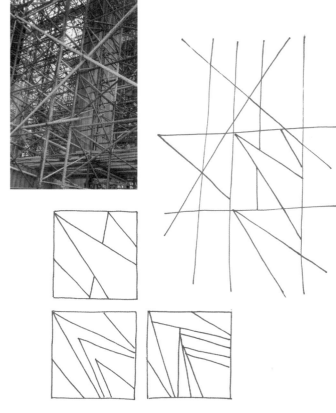

10 Altering the lines, removing some, angling others can change the character of a block.

11 The design workings for *Hot Pink*. The odd angles of scaffolding was the start of the design. The appearance is of an untidy mess but by drawing selected angles and shapes, and organising them into a repeating block it makes them a stunning pattern.

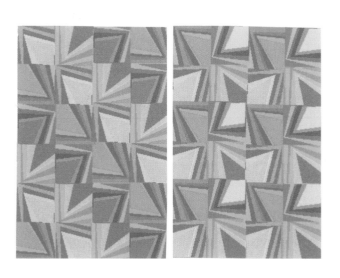

12 Two layouts using the same block as *Hot Pink* but portraying very different characters. Blocks placed in diagonal lines give a stability contrasting with the almost jazzy appearance when the star shape is broken by turning one block in a contrary position.

Hot Pink was developed from the photograph of scaffolding with its odd angles. The wide border of random width strips echoes the shapes and colours in the blocks. The placement of colour was the maker's choice without reference to light and dark tones but the lime green around the off-centre shape and the dark blue are constant. The materials used were American cotton prints. The quilt is foundation pieced and machine quilted along the seam lines of the blocks and round the edge.

Above: Hot Pink
Janet Rae
107 x 135cm (42 x 53in)
(Photo by Michael Wicks)

When she showed this quilt in 'Salute to Quilts' at the Aotea Centre in Auckland in 2003, Catherine Pigeron posed the question: 'Is there anything "original" anymore about Log Cabin patterns?' Having found her inspiration in *A Log Cabin Notebook* by Mary Ellen Hopkins (ME Publications, 1991), Catherine also answered her own question by coming up with a new twist.

Le Fete by Catherine Pigeron, Auckland, NZ.
Cotton, machine pieced, hand appliquéd and quilted.
189cm (74.5in) square.

THE FRAME
Turkey

*Embroidered quilt by Saliha
Berberoglu, Turkey, c.1900
118 x 175cm (45 x 68in)
Courtesy of the maker's
granddaughter, Hayrunissa Magden
(Photo by Ozan Onder)*

*Close-up of embroidered English
table cover, c.1890
162cm (63.5in) square
Photo © Copyright of The Quilters'
Guild of the British Isles*

Quiltmaking in Turkey is a trade traditionally followed by men. Unlike the heavily embroidered quilts by Saliha Berberoglu, however, they are generally wholecloth. Saliha's family roots can be traced to the Balkans and the era of the Ottomans. Saliha lived in the European section of Turkey, however, and it is possible that her choice of the Log Cabin pattern was influenced by Christian missionaries. Although no research has yet been done, other old Log Cabin examples have surfaced in Turkey as prayer rugs using techniques that include Courthouse Steps and Pineapple.

Three embroidered quilts made by Saliha still exist. Two are composed of embroidered squares joined by crochet. The quilt above is folded Log Cabin with a variety of embroidery stitches and ribbon work. It well illustrates the versatility of the Log Cabin block as a vehicle for embellishment. The late 19th century passion for crazy patchwork coincided with the popularity of the Log Cabin pattern, and while many of the Log Cabin quilts were made of cotton, others incorporated the same luxury fabrics as the crazy quilt – silks, satins and velvets. Appliqué, beadwork and painting as well as the whole catalogue of the embroiderer's stitch, were used as embellishment on both types of quilt.

The tablecover on the right, made entirely by hand, is an example of these same decorative techniques applied to a Log Cabin textile originating in England. Black satin ribbon is incorporated in this typical Victorian piece and pearl cotton has been used for the decoration.

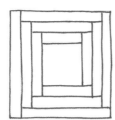

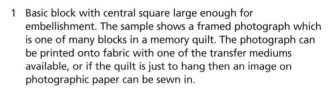

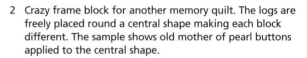

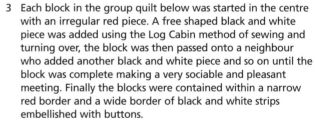

1   Basic block with central square large enough for embellishment. The sample shows a framed photograph which is one of many blocks in a memory quilt. The photograph can be printed onto fabric with one of the transfer mediums available, or if the quilt is just to hang then an image on photographic paper can be sewn in.

2   Crazy frame block for another memory quilt. The logs are freely placed round a central shape making each block different. The sample shows old mother of pearl buttons applied to the central shape.

3   Each block in the group quilt below was started in the centre with an irregular red piece. A free shaped black and white piece was added using the Log Cabin method of sewing and turning over, the block was then passed onto a neighbour who added another black and white piece and so on until the block was complete making a very sociable and pleasant meeting. Finally the blocks were contained within a narrow red border and a wide border of black and white strips embellished with buttons.

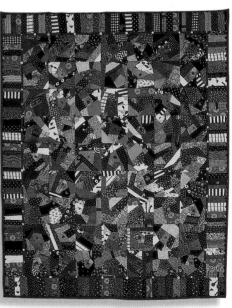

All Buttoned Up Group quilt, Beckenham Quilters, England 178 x 218cm (70 x 86in)

4 A padded Log Cabin frame with a
   centre of rose petals and painting.

5 A large bright floral print
   with range of Amish
   coloured cottons.

6 The floral print surrounded by
   Amish coloured logs with extra
   roses from the print applied to
   appear as if peeping through a
   trellis, and the whole quilt design
   with nine such blocks.

7   Pots of flowers and interesting fabrics from Africa, India and the Far East form the inspiration for Pat Salt's *Flower Arranging*. The holes in the fabrics show where Pat has specially selected particular features for use in the design. She uses the minutest of scraps of fabric to find just the right pieces.

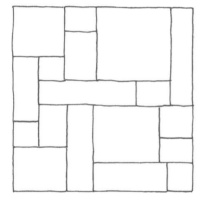

8   Plan of the odd sized Log cabin blocks

9   Sketch for a block.

10 Design for Flower Arranging.

Flower Arranging
Pat Salt, England
74cm square (29in)
(Photo by Michael Wicks)

This entirely hand sewn quilt is one of a series which was inspired by an exhibition of African textiles and a present of fabrics from Africa. The piece comprises a group of small individual appliqué panels, blanket stitched into place through a backing quilt of three layers embellished with buttons and quilted boldly with two rows of contrasting thread.

Labelled Containment of Chaos Marjorie Hoeltzel, United States
Pieced silk neckties and labels 114 x 152.5cm (45 x 60in)

Marjorie Hoeltzel has used the Log Cabin pattern in many different forms. Inspired initially by a quilt made by her grandmother, Marjorie changed the usual cloth foundation to a wire mesh, through which she wove strips of cloth in the Log Cabin pattern. After making a number of these textile constructions to commission, she then experimented with making individual blocks on the mesh and attaching the blocks with metal washers. The move from her large studio to a smaller space made her look again at her Bernina sewing machine and the traditional method of Log Cabin construction. This work, which she calls 'crooked' Log Cabin, well illustrates the influence of crazy patchwork.

GETTING STARTED
Choosing Fabrics

Detail of simple strip quilt, Michigan 1940s
Recycled dress cottons
Collection of Nancy Heusel

Detail of grosgrain ribbon quilt, Cornwall, 1850-1870
162 (64in) square
The Embroiderers' Guild of New South Wales Inc

Fabrics will give your quilt character by their colour, weight and texture: colour will promote a mood, weight will give warmth, and texture will give added interest. What a quilt will be used for will dictate the type of fabric you use. The fabrics on the following three pages are those gathered by the two authors over a life time of sewing.

Striped fabrics bought from the Swedish company Ikea. They were inspired by Scandinavian countryside traditions. They are strong, and suitable for the hard wear needed for a quilt used for camping or boating. ▼

▲ Welsh woollen flannels woven traditionally by Melin Teifi. Working with these wools you realise why the old woollen quilts from Wales are so heavy. In centrally heated houses we do not need this weight in a bed quilt but the wools make a robust wallhanging. See *Two in One* on page 83 where the flannels have been combined with dupion silk.

Recycled blankets dyed blue with indigo and yellow with onion skins. Wool takes vegetable dyes very well. ▼

▲ Sylvania prints from Peru inspired by archaeological treasures and contemporary Indian crafts. They are very fine quality in 100% Pima cotton and can only be purchased in Peru.

▲ Large patterned prints are useful for contrasting with small prints such as the Liberty lawns, and where a dramatic character is required.

▲ Fine quality Liberty lawns from Britain are suitable for light weight quilts. The prints are usually small and the patterns are mostly flower or paisley patterns.

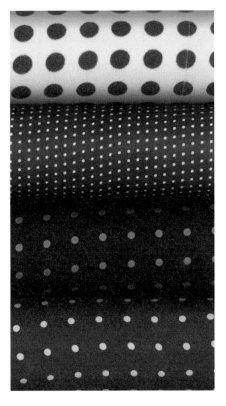

Fabrics from Provence in France are often in small dotty prints or Paisley style, sometimes with borders. They can be purchased in the shops attached to the factories in Provence as can cheaper quality fabrics from local markets. *Window over Provence* on page 35 uses these fabrics. ▼

Over-dying fabrics solves the problem of not finding the right coloured fabric on a shopping expedition. A range of fabrics can be put in the same dye bath: here is one before and after dyeing. Dyeing can be useful when looking for several prints in one colour palette. ▼

◀ Factory off-cuts of silk fabric with dots of various sizes intended for men's ties or cravats. These silks make a warm but light weight quilt. The masculine colours would contrast well with bright floral prints.

Batik prints: one from India with fish batiked over a woven cotton giving a wider range of colours with only one dye bath, one from Holland with cockerels, and an all-over pattern from the Far East. ▼

▲ The colours in prints from India are not precisely placed because of hand printing and painting. This gives the prints a free character of their own.

◀ Dupion silk, usually from China or India, has a gentle rough texture, and comes in a wide range of colours. It cuts easily like paper but will readily fray once cut. *Forest* on page 77 uses dupion silk.

French toiles, usually bought for soft furnishings, have also found their way into the quilter's stash. ▶

Painted and printed kimono silks and indigo blue cottons (see quilt on page 47) are traditionally associated with Japan. But these heavily patterned cottons with gold embellishment also come from that country. ▼

◀ Dutch quiltmakers once had a fondness for using Indian chintz. The reproduction fabrics by Den Haan and Wagenmakers keep the tradition alive.

Handprinted and dyed fabrics lend quilts individuality. The collection by Rawkos features New Zealand images. ▼

▲ Occasionally, a quilter's fabric search can result in indigenous prints. This collection from Australia draws on ancient Maori designs and the country's flora and fauna.

Novelty fabrics like these patriotic prints from the United States are valued by quilters who want to personalize their work – especially if the quilt is intended for a family member or friend. ▶

Sewing Techniques

Wow
Log Cabin Sampler Quilt
Elizabeth Sell, England
160 x 213cm (63 x 86in)

Elizabeth makes an intriguing number of variations on the Log Cabin block in a vibrant primary colour scheme. It shows many geometric ideas strikingly assembled.

The basic technique of a Log Cabin block requires the repeated placing of one strip next to another. The traditional block has strips arranged round a centre square. The colour placement is critical to the look: usually two adjacent sides of the block are in contrast to the other two sides as shown in the illustration on the right.

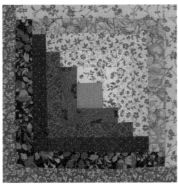

Drawing the Block Pattern

Draft a traditional Log Cabin block by drawing a square (say 20cm or 8in). On the left side of the square, draw a line the width of the required strips (say 2.5cm or 1in) from top to bottom. Draw a second line of the same width from the bottom of the first line to the right side of the square. Draw a third line at the right side of the square to the top. Draw a fourth line connecting the third strip to the first strip. Continue to add lines inside the other strips round the four sides leaving a small central square.

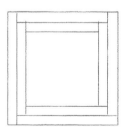
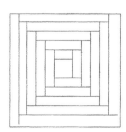

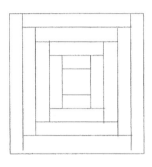

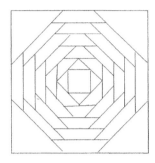

Related blocks are also drawn in this way. Draft the Courthouse Steps block by first drawing lines on opposite sides of the square and then on the remaining sides. Continue to add strips inside the first round of the four sides until the block is completed, leaving a small central square.

More unusual blocks can be drawn using the same method. For example, the Pineapple block is drafted by first drawing lines across the corners to make triangles: lines are then drawn parallel with the sides of the block, then parallel with the triangles. Continue adding the logs in this way until the centre becomes a square.

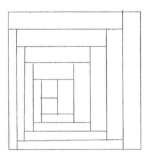
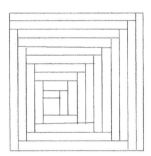
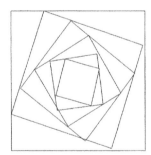

Blocks with varying width strips or e) strips on adjacent sides give the illusi of a curve across the block and move square from its central position. Triangular logs can also suggest curv within the block.

Strips varying in width, from wide to narrow, can give the appearance of (patchwork.

Try experimenting with these ideas to create blocks or to create variations of some of the design ideas in the book.

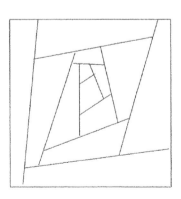

Methods of Sewing

Historically, many different techniques have been used to assemble a Log Cabin block. Modern sewing tools and ingenuity have added others. The technique most used, either with or without a foundation, is to place two strips, right sides together. Sew a seam along the edge leaving a seam allowance, turn over the top strip and press. Place the next strip down, right sides together, sew and turn as before. Continue to add strips in this way.

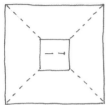  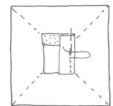   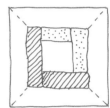

Sewing a Traditional Block on a Foundation Square

To make a traditional Log Cabin block, cut out a backing square the size of the required block with a seam allowance of about 1cm or 1/2in on each side. Mark the centre of this square by folding or drawing the diagonals. Now take the small centre square and contrasting strips, all with seam allowances of 5mm or 1/4in. Place and pin the small square in the centre of the backing square with the corners matching the diagonals. Place a strip of the first colour right sides together with the small square and sew through all three layers on the seam allowance. Turn the strip over, finger press and trim. Going clockwise round the small square place a second strip of the same colour right sides together along the side of the square including the width of the first strip: sew, turn and trim. Continuing round the small square place a third strip in the contrasting colour along the side of the square including the width of the second strip; sew, turn and trim. Next place a fourth strip in the contrasting colour along the side of the square including the width of the third and first strips; sew, turn and trim. Continue in the same direction adding rounds of strips using the contrasting strips on the same sides as in the first round until the backing square is covered. The corners of a completed round should be on the diagonals of the backing square.

Sewing from the Back on Lawn or Interfacing

Cut a square of fine cotton lawn or man-made interlining (Vilene) the size of the block with seam allowance of 1cm or 1/2in all round. Trace a drawing of the block onto one side of the square. This is easier if the drawing and the fabric are held in place with masking tape while tracing. Make a heavy mark with a pencil or a pen, making sure the lines show through and taking care to find out that the marks of the pencil or pen will not seep through the outer fabric when steam ironed. Cut out the small centre square and contrasting strips to correspond with the drawing of the block all with seam allowances of 5mm or 1/4in. Place and pin the small square in the centre on the right side of the foundation square. Place a strip right sides facing with the small square and sew through all three layers on the seam allowance from the back, turn the strip over, finger press and trim. Continuing clockwise, place strips in the same manner as when sewing on a heavier foundation. This method gives perfect results and is for those who like to be very accurate.

Stitch and Tear Method

Use the interfacing method of sewing except substitute thin paper for the foundation square. The paper is torn away when the sewing of the block is complete. Special paper can be bought for this method.

Edge-to-Edge Method

Although not as popular as the foundation method, edge-to-edge does have its place in traditional methods of block assembly and will make considerably lighter weight quilts but quilts that are not so robust. The method of assembly is the same as for the foundation method without using a foundation square. It can be streamlined: sew a series of centre squares butting up to one another to a strip of fabric. Press the seam and cut through the strip where the squares butt. Place these lengthwise onto another strip, sew, press and cut though the strip. Continue to add more strips to the blocks in this way until the blocks are complete. This is similar to Seminole patchwork. The sample below shows a second round of strips started.

Close-up of folded sewing technique,
Woollen sleigh quilt (see page 18)
Norway 1850-1870
170 x 210cm (67 x 83in)
(Photograph by Joan Foster)

Folded Strips on a Foundation

Many old quilts were made by first folding the strips and then sewing them, in overlapping rows, to a foundation. The method was especially popular with heavy wools, velvets and lighter weight fabrics such as silk which would benefit from a double thickness. The foundation may possibly act as the centre square by just adding folded strips.

The Manx Method

For a method requiring only scissors, needle and thread, try making a Log Cabin block following the tradition practised by quilters on the Isle of Man. One of its chief characteristics is that it introduces a pleat – by folding each successive strip slightly back over the seam. The method is both challenging and fun to experiment with and the results depend on the size of your hand. The size of foundation square is measured by the span of the stretched hand from thumb to little finger with a bit added for seam allowance; the centre square by the length of the middle finger; and the width of the strips by measuring from the base of the thumb nail to the base of the thumb. The seam allowance is the width of the little fingernail. The strips are sewn down in the same order as in a traditional block except that two thirds of each strip is folded back making a tuck. This patchwork was often done in poor light and the tuck hid a roughly sewn seam. The blocks were joined together often with no backing to the quilt. The illustration right shows a block using old blanket fabric dyed with indigo and onion skins.

Decorative Machine Stitched Method

This method produces a very lightweight quilt and is best made with dress cottons. Draw the block onto the top of a cotton foundation square. Cut out the pieces precisely with no seam allowance. Place face up on the foundation the first log next to the centre square. Select a wide decorative machine stitch and a contrasting coloured thread and sew across the two butting edges. Place the next log and repeat. Continue adding logs in this way until the square is covered. Join the blocks by butting one up to another with a strip of foundation fabric beneath and stitch together. The blocks may be used as a bedspread or sandwiched with wadding and backing fabric to make a quilt. The top will stand up to gentle washing. See sample 6 on page 44.

Other Styles of Log Cabin Blocks

The methods described here may be used for any block. Strips may be added in a different order such as in the Courthouse Steps block in which the strips are added on opposite sides of the square first followed by the strips on the other opposite sides.

Try making different shaped blocks: starting with a centre triangle will result in a triangular block: an octagon shaped block will need square blocks between to tessellate.

The Roman Stripes and Rail Fence blocks use sets of logs sewn by the simple technique of stitching and turning. The finished blocks are turned against each other to make the patterns.

 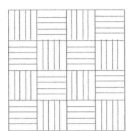 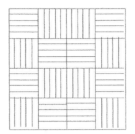 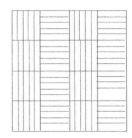

 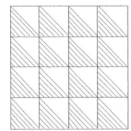 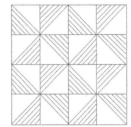 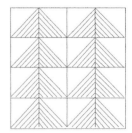

The impression of crazy Log Cabin can be obtained by sewing on logs of varying straight shapes freely.

A double sided Log Cabin block is worked using the edge-to-edge method. Sew the back and front strips on at the same time. A strip of interlining or wadding may be inserted with each

added strip to give the padded look. Assemble the blocks using the quilt-as-you-go method (see page 112).

The diagonal line across the Log Cabin block can be made to appear curved by sewing on more strips on two adjacent sides of the block or by adding wider strips. See the quilt on page 53.

Other curves can be made using tapering triangles and are best sewn from the back using the foundation method.

Woven logs stitched to a foundation would imitate the ways the Egyptians made patterns while binding mummies. See the woven block on page 63.

Assembling the Quilt

Quilting the Whole Piece

Decide on the layout of the blocks and an order for sewing them together. Avoid sewing round corners by stitching in a series of rows or rectangles. To join, place two adjacent blocks right sides facing, sew them together along the seam line and press. The seams may be pressed to one side or open. Open seams spread the weight of the fabric. Continue to sew blocks together into rows and then rows together, or into rectangles and then rectangles together. Straight borders can be added on two opposite sides followed by the other two sides.

To make the quilt sandwich you will need a backing and an interlining slightly larger than the top of the quilt. Place the backing face down on a flat surface making sure it is absolutely flat, keeping it in place with pins or masking tape. Place the interlining flat down on the backing and then place the quilt top face up on the interlining making sure that it is flat and centrally placed. Pin the layers together in one direction so that if the fabric moves it will not wrinkle. Tack across the sandwich in one direction in rows that are approximately 7.5cm (3in) apart followed by rows at right angles to the first. The quilt sandwich is ready to be quilted.

'Quilt-as-You-Go'

This method of assembly is useful for those who have not the space for a large quilting frame and for those who want to handle the weight of the quilt as little as possible. Sections of the quilt are assembled and finally the whole quilt completed.

Join the blocks into manageable sections. Cut out a backing and an interlining (wadding) the size of the section. To assemble, place the backing face down on a table with the interlining on top and then the pieced section. Pin these three layers together systematically and then tack them first in one direction and then at right angles in rows

approximately 5cm (2in) apart. Quilt this section leaving the very edge not quilted to allow for joining the sections together. To join the sections together first pin back the backing and the interlining of the section to be joined. Pin the top sections together face to face and seam. Press the seam open with care. Trim the interlinings sections so that they butt up to one another and ladder stitch together. Lay down one of the backing sections with the other one to form a hem and stitch in place. Join all the sections together in this way planning it so that you do not have to join round a corner. Any borders may be added on using this method. Finally these sections may be quilted (see below).

Alternatively the blocks may be made into a quilt sandwich as the blocks are sewn. Work as if sewing on a foundation but replacing the foundation with backing fabric and wadding. Sew through all layers. The tedious part of this is sewing in the thread ends to keep the back neat. Join the blocks as above.

Quilting

The quilts in this book are made from many pieces and the stitching needed is simply to hold the sandwich together or to emphasize the pattern of the piecing. The quilting may follow the lines of the pieces or the lines of the patterns made by the piecing or an all over pattern such as repeated zig-zag or undulating lines across the quilt. Quilting may be by hand or machine.

For hand quilting use one of the many quilting threads on the market in a colour to support or to contrast with your patterns. Take a thread about 30cm (12in) long and as small a quilting needle as you can manage. Make a knot in the end of the thread, put the needle into the quilt sandwich bringing it up where you intend to start quilting and pull the knot into the quilt sandwich. Take one or more stitches onto the needle through all layers and pull the thread through. Continue this running quilting stitch until the thread is used up, put another knot in the thread

close to the quilt surface, pull it into the sandwich and trim off the end. Many quilters choose to use a frame, either a hoop or a bigger frame, but the suggested amount of tacking is sufficient to hold the sandwich together while quilting without using a frame.

Machine quilting takes a little time to master. Make trial pieces to practise on. A full sized quilt is cumbersome so the smaller sections in the quilt-as-you-go method are easier to manage.

Knotting

Log Cabin quilts are quite heavy if made with a foundation fabric and knotting may be a preferred method of keeping the quilt sandwich together. It is quicker than quilting. The quilt will need knots at least every 20cm (8in). They can be placed regularly or in sympathy with the pattern of the blocks. A knot consists of a stitch taken through all layers, a second stitch made on the same spot, the ends of the thread tied in a reef knot and cut off not too short, about 2.5cm (1in). The thread used can be colourful and decorative or chosen to tone in with the colour of the quilt. The thread should be strong, as it will take considerable strain. For decoration, embellishments such as buttons and tassels may be added into the knot. The Welsh quilt on page 61 has decorative red knots.

Finishing the Edge

The edge of the quilt may be finished in several ways. It can be bound with a straight or bias binding. The front can be turned over on to the back and hemmed or the back to the front. The front may be turned over the interlining and the back turned under to butt with the top and then hemmed in place. Decoration such as a covered cord, rickrack, lace or patchwork shapes may be added into the final hem. Look at the quilts throughout the book for ideas.

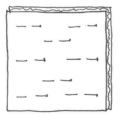
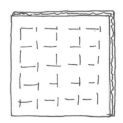
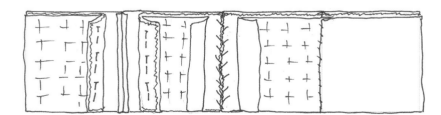

'Quilt-as-You-Go'

Embellishments

Embellishments help give character to a quilt. Illustrated here are a variety of ideas that may be either sewn into the seam or applied to the surface. There are ribbons, braids, lace, buttons, tassels, knots, bows, sequins, Indian shisha glass, beads, safety pins, threads and charms. Some of them may be old perhaps evoking memories. Some may be new perhaps following a theme such as flowers for the feminine touch or hearts for a wedding. Some may be home-made: beads made from coloured threads, threads coloured specially to suit the work, self covered buttons, modelled and painted buttons, tassels made to match and bows to add a pretty touch.

Two pieces of patchwork illustrate the use of ribbon and lace. Several quilts show embellishments earlier in the book. They are tassels on *The Secret Garden* on page 65, prairie points added into the seams of *Barbican* on page 78, buttons supporting the flower shapes in *Flower Arranging* on page 101 and small orange knots on *Jewel Kelim* on page 45

Feather stitched quilt from Guernsey, c.1920
71 x 86.5cm (28 x 34in)
National Trust of Guernsey

The fabrics in this Furrows quilt range from the late 19th century to the 20th but the embroidery embellishment is unusual for the period. The quilt was made using folded strips applied to four inch squares which were then backed by a printed cotton of roses in shades of pink, mauve, yellow and white.

Family Album
Silvia Momesso, Italy
Machine pieced silk and cotton,
hand dyed and printed backing
116 x 128cm (46 x 50.5in)

Individual Log Cabin squares have been allocated to family
members and their interests by the maker who has encapsulated
plastic and any other items within each block. Among the non-
traditional embellishments are guitar strings and a pick; a small
CD Rom; cooking spices; coloured hair-grips; red ribbon and
transparent candy or sweet wrappers to simulate stage lights.

Quilt Borders

The simplest and easiest form of border is a straight strip or a series of strips. Look how the simple strip on *The Changing Tide* on page 53 is sympathetic in colour and width with the whole quilt. It needs no more. Adding strips round side after side, like adding logs to a block, echoes the squareness of the construction of the blocks. Mitred corners are best used only where they relate to something within the quilt design. Similarly the width of the strips should relate to the blocks. Let the patterns of the blocks suggest the border. The borders on each edge do not have to be the same width or even the same number of strips. *Window over Provence* on page 35 illustrates this point.

A border may merely be suggested by making the edge blocks a different shade or the central square of the edge block a different colour. Dominant final logs of blocks can also suggest a border.

A series of squares could make a border. *A Year in the Garden* on page 66 has such a border. The squares relate in size to some of the central squares and the colour of the border continues the suggestion of the diagonal.

Another idea would be to make a border of short strips at right angles to the quilt. The strips could be the size of one of the logs in the blocks or made from crazy logs. *Hot Pink* on page 95 is an example of this.

Borders
Janet Rae
89 x 109cm (35 x 43in)

A quilt of three borders showing seven traditional blocks each of which would make a bold statement on the edge of a quilt.

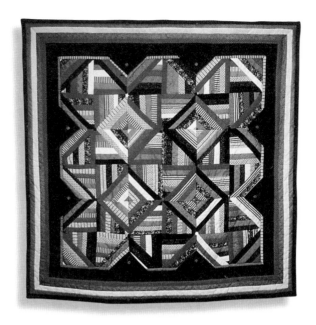

A few ideas for borders. Design your own to match the quilt.

Inside, Outside, Upside-down
Sylvia Critcher, England
203 x 203cm (80 x 80in)

A quillow, a quilt that folds away into a pillow, with an interesting border. Sylvia cleverly adds extra half blocks into the seam of one of the border strips. These half blocks have been lined and are free to lie flat over the strip border or be buttoned back over the quilt giving a completely different character to the quilt.

Milliner's quilt
Edging points on quilt, Scotland c.1860
158 x 191cm (62 x 75in)
National Trust of Scotland, Angus Folk Museum

The various ribbons and silk scraps, left over from hat making in the shop of Miss Jane Yeaman of Forfar, were used to make this quilt with an octagon centre.

Embroidered edge
Scalloped and embroidered edge
of a white cross, Scotland c.1880
203 x 203cm (80 x 80in)
Ceres Folk Museum, Fife

A dramatic Turkey Red quilt with white crosses has an embroidered border of white flowers. The red scalloped edges have been outlined with white satin stitch.

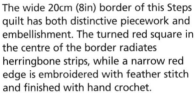

The wide 20cm (8in) border of this Steps quilt has both distinctive piecework and embellishment. The turned red square in the centre of the border radiates herringbone strips, while a narrow red edge is embroidered with feather stitch and finished with hand crochet.

Lace edge
Herringbone-style border with
crochet edge, Scotland c.1870
187 x 201cm (73.5 x 79in)
Ceres Folk Museum, Fife

Off centre Log Cabin with border,
Nicholes Wallace, Australia
c.1895
234 x 236cm (92 x 93in)
National Pioneer Women's Hall of
Fame, Alice Springs

Many Log Cabin quilts are made without a border but this fine Light and Dark layout has been enhanced by a wide border of pieced wedges.

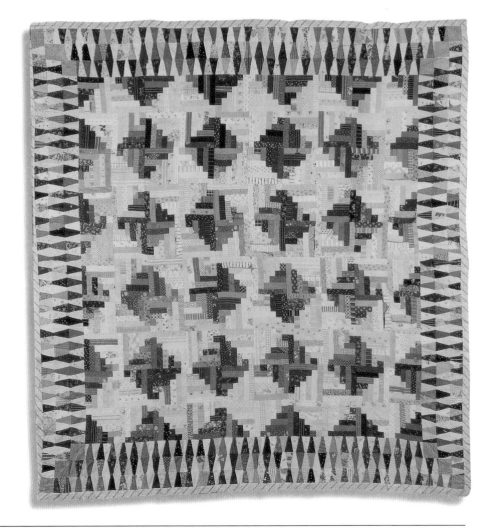

SELECT BIBLIOGRAPHY

Atwater, Mary M. *The Shuttle-craft Book of American Hand-weaving*. New York: The Macmillan Company, 1928; 6th printing 1966.

Bain, George. Celtic *Art. The Methods of Construction*. London: Constable, 1982.

Bennett, Margaret. *Oatmeal & the Catechism. Scottish Gaelic Settlers in Quebec*. Edinburgh: John Donald, 1998.

Brackman, Barbara. *Clues in the Calico*. McLean, Va: EPM Publications Inc,1989.

Clark, Ricky; Knepper, George W; and Ronsheim, Ellice. *Quilts in Community*. Ohio's Traditions. Nashville: Rutledge Hill Press, 1991.

Colby, Avril. *Quilting*. London: B.T. Batsford, 1972.

Conroy, Mary. *300 Years of Canada's Quilts*. Toronto: Griffin House, 1975.

Foster, Joan. *Gamle Tekstiler: Lappeteknikk. Applikasjon*. Quilting. Halden, Norway: N.W. Damm & Son, 2002.

Gero, Annette. *Historic Australian Quilts*. New South Wales: National Trust of Australia, 2000.

Glüsing, Birgit. *Gammelt Dansk* (Old Danish) *Patchwork*. Copenhagen: Glüsing Bøger, 2003.

Ikram, Salima & Dodson, Aidan. *The Mummy in Ancient Egypt: Equipping the Dead for Eternity*. London,Thames and Hudson, 1998.

Heyerdahl, Thor. *Early Man and the Ocean. The beginning of navigation and seaborne civilizations*. London: George Allen & Unwin Ltd, 1978.

Jones, Owen. *The Grammar of Ornament*. London: Omega Books, 1987 (reprint of volume first published in 1856).

Kauffmann-Doig, Federico. *Ancestors of the Incas. The Lost Civilizations of Peru*. Exhibition Catalogue 1998. Wonders. The Memphis International Cultural Series in association with PromPeru and the Instituto Nacional de Cultura del Peru.

Ling, Roger. *Ancient Mosaics*. London: British Museum Press, 1998.

Manning, Jenny. *Australia's Quilts: A Directory of Patchwork Treasures*. Hunters Hill, NSW: AQD Press, 1999.

McKendry, Ruth. *Quilts and Other Bed Coverings in the Canadian Tradition*. Toronto: Van Nostrand Reinhold Ltd, 1979.

Moonan, An. *Quilts, the Dutch Tradition*. Arnhem: Nederlands Openluchtmuseum, 1992.

Quilters' Guild. *Quilt Treasures. The Quilters' Guild Heritage Search*. London: Deirdre McDonald Books, 1995.

Rae, Janet. *Quilts of the British Isles*. London, Constable; New York: E.P. Dutton, 1987. London: Deirdre McDonald Books, 1996 (reprint).

Ramsay, Bets and Waldvogel, Merikay. *The Quilts of Tennessee: Images of Domestic Life Prior to 1930*. Nashville: Rutledge Hill Press, 1986.

Rolfe, Margaret. *Patchwork Quilts in Australia*. Richmond, Victoria: Greenhouse Publications Pty Ltd, 1987.
– *Australian Quilt Heritage*. Rushcutters Bay: J.B. Fairfax Press, 1988.

Seligman, G. Saville and Hughes, Talbot. *Domestic Needlework, Its Origins and Customs Throughout the Centuries*. London:Country Life; Paris: Firmin-Didot et Cie,1926.

Sutton, Ann. *The Structure of Weaving*. London: Hutchinson, 1982.

Tarrant, Naomi. *Textile Treasures.* Edinburgh: National Museums of Scotland Publishing Ltd, 2001.

Taylor, John H. *Death & the Afterlife in Ancient Egypt.* London: The British Museum Press, 2001.

Valentine, Fawn. *Echoes from the Hills: West Virginia Quilts and Quiltmakers.* Athens: Ohio University Press, 2000.

von Gwinner, Schnuppe. *The History of the Patchwork Quilt.* West Chester, Pa: (English edition) Schiffer Publishing Ltd, 1988.

Weldon's Encyclopaedia of Needlework. London: The Waverley Book Co Ltd, 1939.

Welters, Linda (ed) and Ordonez, Margaret T. *Down by the Old Mill Stream: Quilts in Rhode Island.* Kent, Ohio: Kent State University Press, 2000.

Wettre, Asa. *Old Swedish Quilts.* (Translated from Swedish by Kristine Fredriksson) Loveland, Colorado: Interweave Press, 1995.

Wilson, Eva. *Ancient Egyptian Designs.* London: The British Museum Press, 2000.
– *Roman Designs.* London: The British Museum Press,1999.

Studies

'The Prince Edward Island Heirloom Quilt Survey: A Progress Report' by Sherrie F. Davidson in *Patchwords 1992 & Patchwords 1994* (Vol 1 and 2 of the Research Papers of the Canadian Quilt Study Group, Ed. Nancy Cameron Armstrong.

'Characteristics of Missouri–German Quilts' by Suellen Meyer. *Uncoverings* 1984. Research Papers of American Quilt Study Group.

'Quiltmaking in Counties Antrim and Down: Some Preliminary Findings from the Ulster Quilt Survey' by Valerie Wilson. *Uncoverings* 1991.

INDEX

ACKNOWLEDGEMENTS

■

The best 'fringe' benefit of patchwork and quilting is the opportunity for international networking and friendship. Nowadays, quilters can travel almost anywhere in the world and find something of interest – a textile museum, a quilt show, a shop with unusual fabric or a fellow 'addict'. It is this very network (and the marvel of email) that has made this book possible. Many quilters and friends around the globe have generously supported our project and we are indeed grateful.

We should particularly like to thank the contemporary quiltmakers, quilt historians, collectors and textile artists working in other disciplines who shared information and often photographs. These included: in Australia, Judy Hooworth, Barbara Macey, Dianne Finnegan and Margaret Rolfe; in Belgium, Rita Bos-Croes; in Canada, Ruth McKendry; in Denmark, Birgit Glüsing; in Estonia, Anni Kreem; in England, Ron Simpson, Ann Sutton, Vine McGill, Pat Salt, Nikki Tinkler, Inger Milburn, Beckenham Quilters, Sheila Yale, Pat Taylor, Patty Murphy, Mavis Haslem, Sylvia Critcher, and Elizabeth Sell; in Germany, Bridget-Ingram Bartholomaus; in Holland, An Moonan; in Ireland, Ann Fleeton; in Italy, Silvia Momesso; in Japan, Akemi Narita, Reiko Hatakeyama, Chiyo Nakagawa, Keiko Torii; in New Zealand, Catherine Pigeron; in Northern Ireland, Irene MacWilliam; in Norway, Joan Foster; in Scotland, Angela Chisholm, Sheena Norquay and Lindsay Hall; in Sweden, Asa Wettre; in the United States, Marjorie Hoeltzel, Nancy Strong and Nancy Heusel; in Wales, Jen Jones. Nor can we forget the valuable help of the two Scottish readers, Hazel Mills and Jenny Carter, who commented on the historical text and the professional support of book designer Caleb Rutherford and photographer Michael Wicks.

Since we were unable, personally, to travel around the world in our quest for the Log Cabin story, the support of museum staff was of the utmost importance. Those who come in for a special accolade include, in North America, Christina Bates, The Canadian Museum of Civilization, Quebec and Sandy Staebell, Western Kentucky University. In Scotland, support was provided by Susan Payne, Perth Museum & Art Gallery; Ray Louden, Angus Folk Museum; and Helen Armitage, Ceres Folk Museum, as well as the National Museums of Scotland and the National Library of Scotland. We should also like to single out Valerie Wilson, Ulster Folk and Transport Museum in Cultra, Northern Ireland; Gillian Lenfestey, the National Trust of Guernsey; Yvonne Cresswell, Manx National Heritage; Joan Thrussell, Cregneash Village Folk Museum, Isle of Man; The Quilters' Guild of the British Isles and Tina Fenwick Smith and Bridget Long.

Last but certainly not least, we owe thanks for the patience and good humour of the two 'who stood and waited' (and also provided the necessary practical backup) during various forays around the country: it is our good fortune that Gilbert Travis and Bill Rae have long experience as quilting partners and are also well versed in the challenges accompanying book writing and production.

Janet Rae and Dinah Travis

Rose Trellis
Irene MacWilliam, Northern Ireland
Foundation pieced, hand-dyed cottons
64cm square (24in)

Despite its small size, this wallhanging of crazy pieced strips, contains 1,116 pieces!

ABOUT THE AUTHORS

■

Making Connections is a unique venture into design history and inspiration for experienced textile enthusiasts who want to explore and push forward their individual development. The collaborators, Janet Rae and Dinah Travis, both well known quiltmakers and authors in the UK, came to the task with complementary skills and experience.

Dinah Travis trained in painting, printing, design and textiles at art school and taught art in secondary education in Kent. Later she taught patchwork and design to City and Guild students at Bromley Adult Education College. With fellow teacher Pat Salt, she also designed and created a correspondence course on patchwork and quilting which has students from around the world. She has published three books based on her teaching: *The Sampler Quilt Workbook* (Batsford, 1990); *The Appliqué Quilt* (Batsford 1993); and *The Miniature Quilt Book* (Batsford 1998).

Janet Rae, a quilt historian and lecturer, is author of *Quilts of the British Isles* (Constable, UK and EP Dutton, US, 1987) and co-author of *Traditional Crafts of Scotland* (Chambers 1988). Her professional background is in newspaper journalism and book and magazine publishing, and she has written numerous feature articles and reviews about textiles and other crafts for journals in many countries.

The authors are both active members of the Quilters' Guild of the British Isles and have held various posts in that organisation: Janet is a former Heritage Officer and Dinah is a former Keeper of the Guild's heritage quilt collection. Both were involved in the three-year British quilt documentation programme in the early 1990s and both contributed to the resultant book, *Quilt Treasures, The Quilters' Guild Heritage Search* (Deirdre McDonald Books, 1995).